Biological Report 85(15)
December 1984

TAMPA BAY ENVIRONMENTAL ATLAS

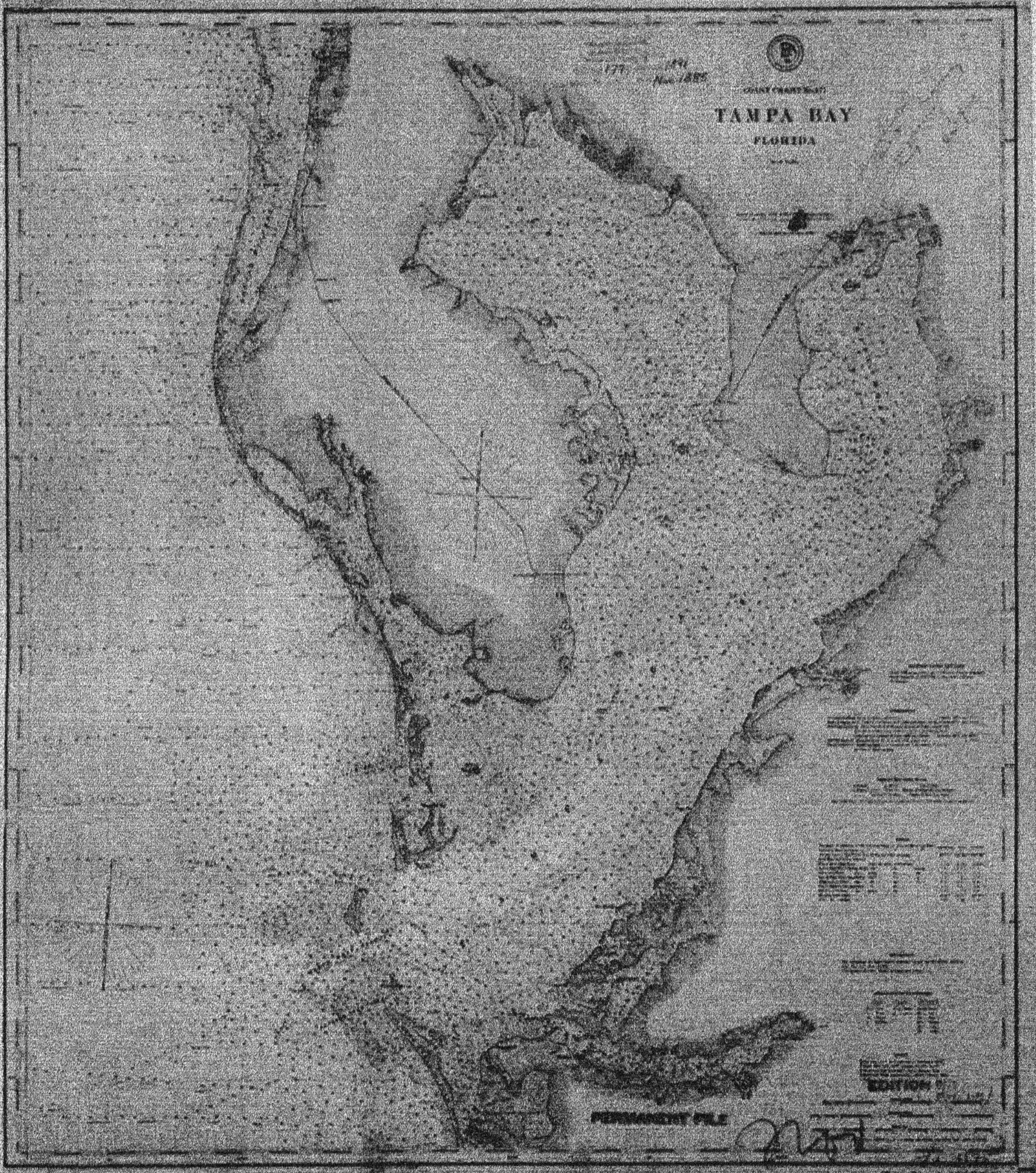

Fish and Wildlife Service

U.S. Department of the Interior

Cover map:
Nautical chart of Tampa Bay, Florida, 1885, from the files of the
National Archives, Record Group 23, Chart 177, 6th ed. August
1900.

U.S. FISH & WILDLIFE SERVICE
National Wetlands Research Center
NASA - Slidell Computer Complex
1010 Gause Boulevard
Slidell, LA 70458

Biological Report 85(15)
December 1984

TAMPA BAY ENVIRONMENTAL ATLAS

By
J. Thomas Kunneke
and
Thomas F. Palik
Martel Laboratories, Inc.
7100 30th Avenue North
St. Petersburg, FL 33710

This study was sponsored by the
Fish and Wildlife Service
U.S. Department of the Interior

Project Officer

James Johnston
National Coastal Ecosystems Team
U.S. Fish and Wildlife Service
NASA/Slidell Computer Complex
1010 Gause Boulevard
Slidell, LA 70458

Performed for

National Coastal Ecosystems Team
Division of Biological Services
Research and Development
Fish and Wildlife Service
U.S. Department of the Interior
Washington, DC 20240

Library of Congress Cataloging-in-Publication Data

Kunneke, J. Thomas.
    Tampa Bay environmental atlas.

    (Biological report / Fish and Wildlife Service ;
85 (15))
    "Project officer, James Johnston, National Coastal
Ecosystems Team, U.S. Fish and Wildlife Service,
NASA/Slidell Computer Complex."
    Supt. of Docs. no.: I 49.89/2:85(15)
    1. Coastal ecology--Florida--Tampa Bay Region--Maps.
2. Coastal zone management--Florida--Tampa Bay Region--
Maps. 3. Tampa Bay Region (Fla.)--Maps. I. Palik,
Thomas F. II. Martel Laboratories. III. National
Coastal Ecosystems Team (U.S.) IV. U.S. Fish and
Wildlife Service. V. Series: Biological report
(Washington, DC) ; 85-15.
G1317.T3C6K8 1986   912'.13339164'0916364   86-600552

This report and the accompanying atlas should be cited:

Kunneke, J.T., and T.F. Palik. 1984. Tampa Bay environmental atlas. U.S.
    Fish Wildl. Serv. Biol. Rep. 85(15). 73 pp. + 38 separate maps (A1 through
    B21).

PREFACE

The purpose of the Tampa Bay Environmental Atlas is to compile existing biological and water resource data for the Tampa Bay ecosystem and map these data at a scale of 1:24,000. The atlas was compiled in conjunction with the 1982, 1972, and 1952 wetland land-use mapping of the Tampa Bay area, which is also at a scale of 1:24,000. The Tampa Bay Environmental Atlas consists of composited information overlain on 18 biological and 20 water resource base maps to produce a total of 38 maps, and an accompanying map narrative. Federal, State and local decision-makers will be able to use this atlas and its accompanying map narrative for coastal planning and management of the wetland areas within the Tampa Bay ecosystem study area.

This project was conducted under Contract FWS 14-16-0009-83-002. Funding was provided by the U.S. Fish and Wildlife Service.

Any questions regarding this publication should be directed to:

Information Transfer Specialist
National Coastal Ecosystems Team
U.S. Fish and Wildlife Service
NASA/Slidell Computer Complex
1010 Gause Boulevard
Slidell, Louisiana 70458

CONVERSION TABLE

Metric to U.S. Customary

Multiply	By	To Obtain
millimeters (mm)	0.03937	inches
centimeters (cm)	0.3937	inches
meters (m)	3.281	feet
kilometers (km)	0.6214	miles
square meters (m^2)	10.76	square feet
square kilometers (km^2)	0.3861	square miles
hectares (ha)	2.471	acres
liters (1)	0.2642	gallons
cubic meters (m^3)	35.31	cubic feet
cubic meters	0.0008110	acre-feet
milligrams (mg)	0.00003527	ounces
grams (g)	0.03527	ounces
kilograms (kg)	2.205	pounds
metric tons (t)	2205.0	pounds
metric tons	1.102	short tons
kilocalories (kcal)	3.968	British thermal units
Celsius degrees	$1.8(°C) + 32$	Fahrenheit degrees

U.S. Customary to Metric

Multiply	By	To Obtain
inches	25.40	millimeters
inches	2.54	centimeters
feet (ft)	0.3048	meters
fathoms	1.829	meters
miles (mi)	1.609	kilometers
nautical miles (nmi)	1.852	kilometers
square feet (ft^2)	0.0929	square meters
acres	0.4047	hectares
square miles (mi^2)	2.590	square kilometers
gallons (gal)	3.785	liters
cubic feet (ft^3)	0.02831	cubic meters
acre-feet	1233.0	cubic meters
ounces (oz)	28.35	grams
pounds (lb)	0.4536	kilograms
short tons (ton)	0.9072	metric tons
British thermal units (Btu)	0.2520	kilocalories
Fahrenheit degrees	$0.5556(°F - 32)$	Celsius degrees

CONTENTS

FIGURES

TABLES

ACKNOWLEDGMENTS

This atlas was funded by the National Coastal Ecosystems Team, Division of Biological Services, Fish and Wildlife Service, U.S. Department of the Interior, Washington, D.C.

The authors sincerely appreciate the critical reviews of the first draft of this report which were provided by the Tampa Port Authority, Office of Environmental Affairs: William K. Fehring; U.S. Geological Survey, Tampa: Carl Goodwin; Office of the Governor, Tallahassee: Libby Herland; Florida Department of Environmental Regulation, Tampa: Ralph Moon; Tampa Bay Regional Planning Council, St. Petersburg: Michael McKinley; Florida Department of Natural Resources, St. Petersburg: Barbara Harris; U.S. Fish and Wildlife Service, Vero Beach: Joe Carroll; University of South Florida, Engineering Department, Tampa: Bernard Ross; Mangrove Systems, Inc., Tampa: Roy Lewis III; U.S. Fish and Wildlife Service, Jacksonville: David Wesley; Gulf of Mexico. Minerals Management Service, New Orleans: Larry Handley. We would also like to acknowledge the assistance of the staff at the National Coastal Ecosystems Team including Joyce Rodberg, Daisy Singleton, Dianne Cain, Anita McKelroy, Gaye Farris, Rob Brown, and Sue Lauritzen.

Martel Laboratories gratefully acknowledges the input and advice from the many individuals and organizations which supplied data for this atlas.

1. INTRODUCTION

1.1 GENERAL

The Tampa Bay Environmental Atlas is a comprehensive large-scale atlas of the biological and water resources of the Tampa Bay area. The study area is the greater Tampa Bay coastal region within the following 21 U.S. Geological Survey 1:24,000-scale quadrangle maps (Figure 1):

Oldsmar	Riverview
Citrus Park	Pass-A-Grille Beach
Clearwater	Cockroach Bay
Safety Harbor	Ruskin
Gandy Bridge	Egmont Key
Tampa	Anna Maria
Brandon	Palmetto
Seminole	Parrish
St. Petersburg	Bradenton
Port Tampa	Lorraine
Gibsonton	

The atlas is being produced in conjunction with the 1982, 1972, and 1952 wetland land-use mapping of the Tampa Bay area, which is also being mapped at a scale of 1:24,000. The Tampa Bay Environmental Atlas consists of composited information overlain on 18 biological and 20 water resource base maps to produce 38 maps and this accompanying map narrative report. Map numbers A19, A20, A21, and B19 were not printed due to lack of data on the resources of this area. The data used in the production of this atlas meet all cartographic standards and specifications outlined by the U.S. Fish and Wildlife Service. Previously or newly acquired map data and collateral information have been compiled to produce this atlas.

The topics included within this map narrative are biological resources and water resources.

Federal, State, and local decisionmakers will be able to use this atlas for coastal planning and management of the wetland areas within the Tampa Bay ecosystem study area.

Included within the Tampa Bay Environmental Atlas are Tampa Bay (200.4 mi^2), Hillsborough Bay (40.4 mi^2), Old Tampa Bay (78.3 mi^2), Boca Ciega Bay (26.9 mi^2), St. Joseph Sound (53.2 mi^2), and the northern portion of Sarasota Bay (55.6 mi^2). The average depth of these waters is 11.4 ft. (mhw) (McNulty et al. 1972; Lewis and Whitman 1984).

1

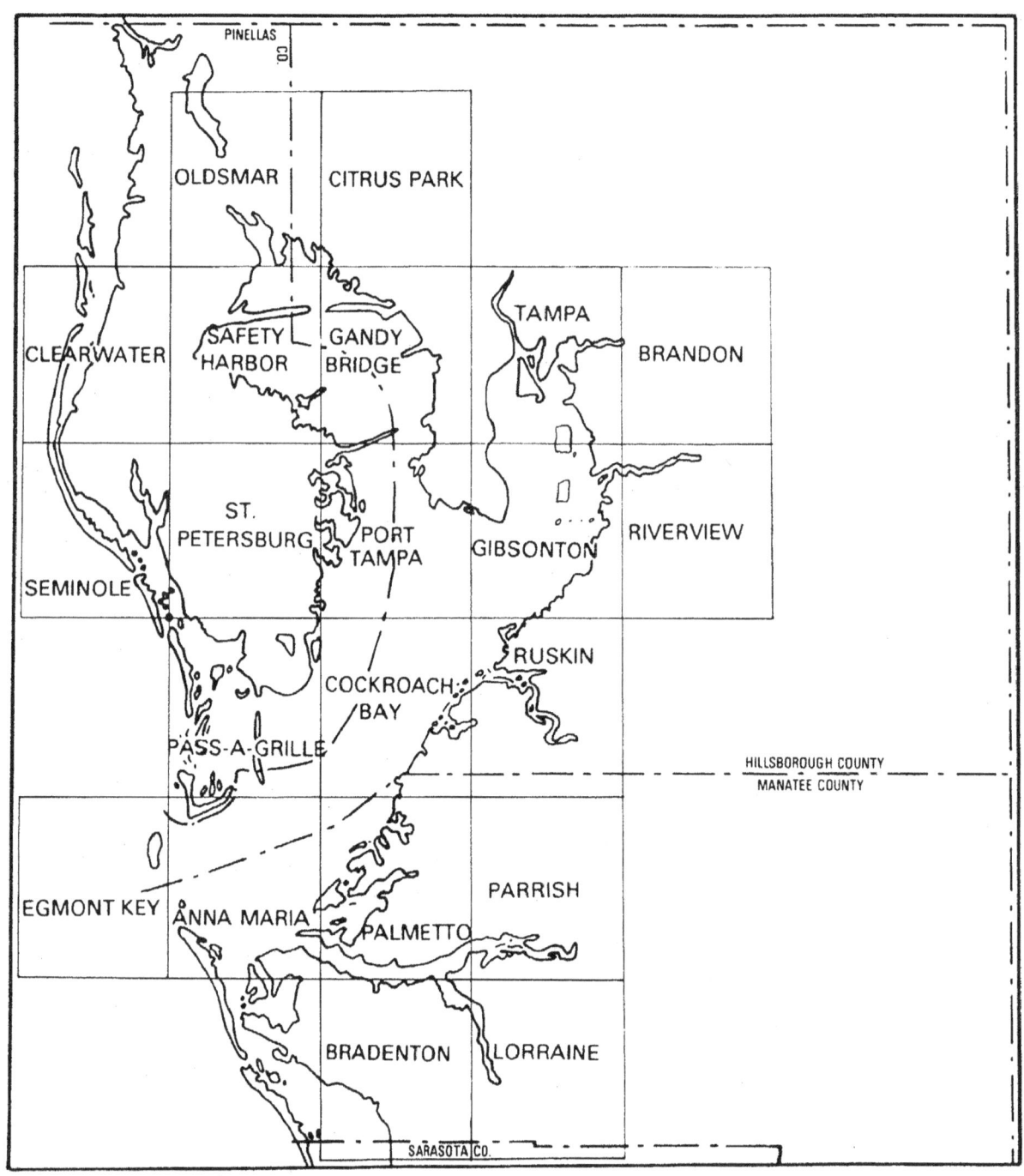

Figure 1. Quadrangles included in Tampa Bay environmental atlas.

1.2 BIOLOGICAL RESOURCES

The Tampa Bay ecosystem is part of the Outer Coastal Plain Ecological Province according to R.G. Bailey (1978). The Outer Coastal Plain Ecological Province is an area of gentle slopes with numerous rivers and creeks. Swamps, marshes, and lakes are abundant in the region and support a wide variety of animal life. The Hillsborough, Alafia, Little Manatee, and Manatee Rivers all empty into Tampa Bay, which is a drowned river valley.

Biological map topics are approved shellfish harvest areas, oyster beds, clams, scallops, finfish, shore birds, wading birds, manatee habitat, seagrass beds, and artificial reefs.

1.3 WATER RESOURCES

The topics on the water resource maps include salinity (mapped as specific conductivity), point source discharges, dredge spoil disposal areas, tide stations, water quality, bathymetry, the intertidal zone, sediments (mapped by grain size), tidal currents, and the freshwater-saltwater interface.

2. BIOLOGICAL RESOURCES

2.1 APPROVED SHELLFISH HARVEST AREAS

Approved shellfish harvest areas depicted in the atlas are defined by strict water quality standards and do not show actual extent of shellfish aggregations. Continual monitoring of fecal coliform bacteria levels is conducted by the Florida Department of Natural Resources (FDNR), Bureau of Marine Regulation and Development through the Department's Shellfish Environmental Assessment Section. Shellfish harvest areas are classified as either approved, conditionally approved, prohibited, or unclassified. Approved areas consistently fulfill water quality criteria (a total coliform bacteria of less than 70 colonies per 100-ml sample). Conditionally approved areas also meet water quality standards, but are subject to more frequent localized changes from flooding and urban runoff which reduce water quality. Prohibited areas, which consistently do not fulfill such requirements, are officially prohibited for the harvesting of shellfish. Unclassified areas are not subjected to continual water quality monitoring and are officially unapproved for shellfish harvesting. The classification of all coastal and estuarine waters is subject to change due to water quality standards. Current shellfish harvest status of any particular area can be obtained from county health departments and the local office of the FDNR, Shellfish Environmental Assessment Section, Punta Gorda, Florida, (813) 639-3443.

Shellfish is a broad term applied to many invertebrates. The water quality constraints imposed by shellfish harvest areas are directed at those species of shellfish which filter water to feed, specifically clams and oysters. These filter feeders, eaten in their entirety, have the potential to concentrate pathogens and toxins (Palik and Lewis 1984).

The generalized location of shellfish harvest areas is shown in Figure 2. Total commercial landings by shellfish species for Pinellas, Hillsborugh, and Manatee Counties for 1982 are itemized in Appendix C.

2.2 OYSTER BEDS

The American oyster (Crassostrea virginica) spawns during the late spring and summer, generally from April through October. Larvae are pelagic for 2-3 weeks, then settle and become permanently attached to pilings, red mangrove roots, seawalls, or hard substrate in the form of oyster reefs. They then grow rapidly, provided water flow, temperature, and salinity are favorable. Good water flow not only aids in dispersal of the larvae, but also assures transport of nutrients and removal of wastes. Oysters can tolerate a wide salinity range (10-30 ppt). Temperatures of 25° to 26 °C and salinities of

4

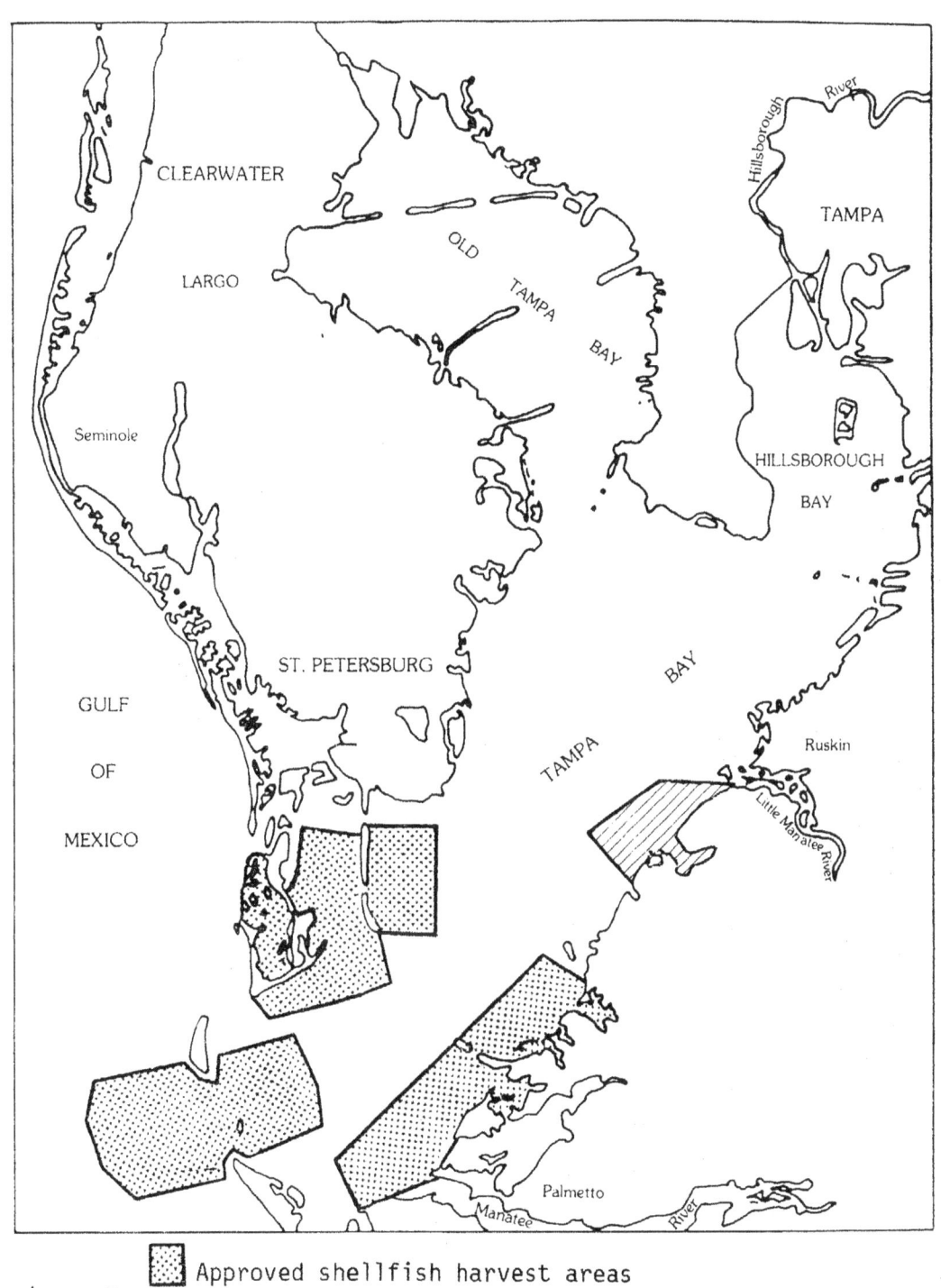

Legend:
☷ Approved shellfish harvest areas

╱ Conditionally approved shellfish harvest areas

Figure 2. Approved shellfish harvest areas in Tampa Bay (Florida Department of Natural Resources 1984).

25 ppt promote optimal growth. Oysters in Florida attain marketable size in about 3 years. Oysters are filter feeders, sorting food by size during ingestion. Phytoplankton, bacteria, and detritus are important foods (McNulty et al. 1972).

In the Tampa Bay study area, this species grows on nearly any suitable substrate such as seawalls and ridge-shaped reefs. The large, naturally occurring aggregations of oysters are depicted on the atlas maps as public oyster beds (Oys-1).

In selected areas, portions of submerged lands within estuaries have been leased by private interests from the State of Florida to grow oysters. These areas appear on the atlas maps as private oyster beds (Oys-2). Certain areas acquired for oyster growing were subsequently closed to shellfish harvesting by the FDNR due to water quality below approved criteria.

Because they are filter feeders, oysters can concentrate micro-organisms and heavy metals as much as several thousandfold; this poses a potential health hazard since oysters are often found in shallow estuaries which may be contaminated with effluent containing pathogenic bacteria and viruses. For this reason, oyster harvesting is regulated according to strict water quality standards. Because estuarine water quality is subject to rapid change, oyster areas must be monitored frequently and may be only conditionally approved. State law prohibits taking oysters between June 1 and August 31. The minimum allowable size for taking oysters is 3 inches as determined by State law. Oysters are not a commercially important shellfish in the Tampa Bay study area; only 132 lb brought in $167 in 1982 (Snell 1984).

2.3 CLAMS

Three species of clams occur in significant abundance in the Tampa Bay study area: the northern quahog (Mercenaria mercenaria), the southern quahog (Mercenaria campechiensis), and the sunray venus clam (Macrocallista nimposa). All are found in estuaries and coastal waters from the mean high tide level to depths of 50 ft and in salinities of 20-35 ppt. Generalized areas of known clam concentrations as determined by Sims and Stokes 1967, Godcharles and Jaap 1973, Tracy 1983, and Sprague 1984 are shown as closed polygons on the individual atlas maps (please see Section 6.1.3).

Clams prefer sandy bottoms in areas of low turbidity (clear water). Too much silt in the water can smother the animals. In bays, clams tend to occur in seagrasses and algal assemblages. The northern quahog did not historically occur on the west coast of Florida, but recent introductions appear to have established successful populations in Tampa Bay. Quahogs spawn between April and August, and sunray venus clams from July through December. Planktonic larvae remain in the water column for about 2 weeks before settling and burrowing into the sediments. Juveniles are subject to predation by the blue crab (Callinectes sapidus). Southern quahogs grow to commercial size rapidly, reaching minimum size in 1 to 1.5 years, while northern quahogs require 2 to 3 years, and sunray venus clams 5 to 6 years. The life expectancy of quahogs can be more than 15 years.

6

Clams are suspension feeders, filtering detritus and micro-organisms from the water column. Thus, they may accumulate toxins and pathogens associated with red tides or polluted water. Areas of Tampa Bay support clam fisheries on a sporadic basis. State law regulates clam harvesting according to water quality standards; also, certain kinds of harvesting equipment (dredges) are prohibited because they cause excessive damage to sensitive areas such as seagrass meadows (Godcharles and Jaap 1973).

Clams are harvested in the Tampa Bay area in waters mostly less than 5 ft by the use of handheld clam rakes which cause little increase in water turbidity (McNulty et al. 1972; Palik and Lewis 1984). Clams are not a commercially important shellfish with only 70 lb bringing in $158 in 1982 (Snell 1984). However, they represent a commercially valuable recreational fishery.

2.4 FINFISH SPAWNING, NURSERY, AND HARVEST AREAS

The sheltered embayments of the estuaries in and around Tampa Bay provide vital habitat for adult and nursery stocks of the commercial and recreational finfish found in the Tampa Bay study area.

Finfish spawning, nursery, and harvest areas are keyed to a species data matrix in the supplemental legend of each biological resource map.

2.4.1 Estuarine-Dependent Fishes

The following finfish descriptions were taken from Palik and Lewis 1984. Landings by fish species can be found in Appendix B.

2.4.1.1 Red drum (Sciaenops ocellatus). Red drum inhabit estuarine and nearshore Gulf of Mexico waters. Spawning occurs in nearshore coastal areas beginning in September and continuing through February. Larvae are transported to estuarine nursery areas by currents, where they remain during the summer, developing into juveniles which leave the estuary with the onset of cold weather. As the fish mature, they apparently prefer to spend more time in the shallow nearshore gulf. Red drum are primarily bottom feeders with a preference for crabs and shrimp. They exhibit secondary midwater and surface feeding. There is a 12-inch minimum size limit on red drum.

2.4.1.2 Spotted seatrout (Cynoscion nebulosus). The spotted seatrout is very closely tied to the estuary. Spawning occurs within the estuary and possibly in those waters immediately adjacent to the mouth of the estuary. South Florida stocks apparently spawn year round with a major peak in the spring and a minor peak in the fall. Essentially nonmigratory, seatrout exhibit a random residential range within the estuary. Tagging studies have shown that most fish move less than 30 mi. Seagrass meadows are the primary habitat for the spotted seatrout.

Each estuary appears to have a unique breeding stock, each stock having slightly different morphological traits. Habitat preference appears to be seagrass beds. Spotted seatrout feed on fish, shrimp, and other crustaceans

7

and become more piscivorous as they mature. A 12-inch minimum size limit is imposed throughout the study area.

2.4.1.3 <u>Snook (Centropomus undecimalis)</u>. Snook are essentially tropical fish and sensitive to cold-induced mortality. Spawning, possibly lunar-induced, occurs at and near tidal passes from late May through July. Eggs and larvae are transported to estuarine and brackish nursery areas by currents. Juveniles live in the upper reaches of the estuary, primarily in brackish streams, ditches, and tidal freshwater creeks. Snook are essentially nonmigratory, but do exhibit a residential range within the estuary and a net movement to the passes during the spawning season. Snook feed on fish and crustaceans. A closed season on snook exists between June 1 and July 31 and between January 1 and February 28. A possession limit of two fish and a minimum size limit of 18 inches have also been imposed. This judicious action has been imposed in an effort to promote recovery of a declining population.

2.4.1.4 <u>Sheepshead (Archosargus probatocephalus)</u>. The sheepshead is a popular sport fish caught along piers, bridges and seawalls of the Tampa Bay area. It is considered an advanced member of the family Sparidae, which is a group of deep bodied perciform fishes that primarily have a tropical distribution. Spawning takes place from March to May along the sandy beaches in the early evening. Juveniles migrate to seagrass areas after hatching. Adult sheepshead generally inhabit areas of rocks, piling, and seawalls in the bays and usually school before spawning just offshore of the major bays. The chief foods for adults are hard mollusks and crustaceans (Mook 1971).

2.4.1.5 <u>Southern flounder (Paralichthys lethostigma)</u>. Spawning occurs offshore in fall and winter when adults migrate from estuarine and coastal nearshore waters. The buoyant eggs usually hatch within 2 days, and larvae move to inshore and estuarine nursery areas. During this time, the symmetric larvae undergo a metamorphosis in which the skull contorts and the right eye moves around to the left of the body. Juveniles typically inhabit shallow estuarine grass beds where they feed largely on marine worms, crustaceans, and fish. Adults are capable of protective coloration changes to blend with the surrounding bottom and feed almost exclusively on fish and crustaceans. The State has imposed an 11-inch minimum size limit on flounders.

2.4.1.6 <u>Florida pompano (Trachinotus carolinus)</u>. Although the exact spawning location is unknown, pompano are considered to spawn offshore, evidenced by the appearance of very early larval forms in offshore gulf waters. The peak of an extended spawning season is from April through June. Rapidly growing juveniles prefer open beach areas where they forage for crustaceans and mollusks. Florida supplies nearly 90% of the U.S. population of pompano, which commands the highest price per pound of any fish in the Southern United States. Florida law prohibits the harvest of pompano less than 9.5 inches long.

2.4.1.7 <u>Striped mullet (Mugil cephalus)</u>. Spawning occurs between October and January in offshore waters. Floating eggs typically hatch within 2 days, and the developing planktonic larvae move into estuarine nursery areas where they remain until sexual maturity, approximately 2 to 3 years. Larvae and small juveniles feed on zooplankton, while juveniles and adults are herbivorous, feeding on diatoms, algae, and benthic detritus. With the

8

exception of the seaward spawning migration in the fall, mullet remain in and are directly dependent on the estuary.

2.4.1.8 <u>Gulf menhaden (Brevoortia patronus)</u>. The gulf menhaden is abundant in the northern Gulf of Mexico, and commercial harvesting efforts are concentrated in that region. Spawning probably takes place in coastal inshore areas. Planktonic larvae are selective carnivores and migrate inshore and enter the estuarine nursery areas as juveniles. Juveniles develop a specialized gill raker-alimentary tract complex with which they feed by nonselective omnivorous filtering. Movement into and established residence in the estuary are an integral part of the menhaden life cycle.

2.4.1.9 <u>Black drum (Pogonias cromis)</u>. Black drum, although not commercially important, are a popular fish among sports fishermen in Tampa Bay. Black drum use Tampa Bay as a nursery in the summer and fall.

2.4.2 <u>Reef Fishes</u>

Groupers and snappers are important to both the recreational and commercial fisheries of the region. Generally, they spawn offshore over the Continental Shelf. Pelagic larvae are transported great distances by oceanic currents. Upon their arrival at inshore, coastal, and estuarine nursery areas, juveniles seek cover and forage for fishes and crustaceans. Typically, as these fish develop, they move offshore. Although inhabitants of other areas, these fish generally seek out structures with some vertical relief, such as wrecks, artificial and coral reefs, rocky areas, holes, and ledges. Most groupers are protogynous hermaphrodites, beginning life as females and transforming into males at around age 5 to 7 years. The State of Florida imposes a 12-inch minimum size on groupers.

2.4.2.1 <u>Red grouper (Epinephelus morio)</u>. Commonly offshore of Tampa Bay, the red grouper spawns in the spring over the Continental Shelf. Juveniles develop in coastal areas and tend to move offshore with age. This is an economically important species in the Tampa Bay study area.

2.4.2.2 <u>Jewfish (Epinephelus itajara)</u>. The jewfish is the largest of the groupers and can attain lengths in excess of 8 ft and weigh over 700 lb. Spawning happens in offshore waters during July and August. Juveniles and young adults inhabit coastal and estuarine seagrass beds and mangroves. Although occasionally occurring inshore, marine jewfish tend to frequent offshore habitats.

2.4.2.3 <u>Gag grouper (Mycteroperca microlepis)</u>. The gag and the red are the major groupers contributing to the commercial and recreational fishery. The gag is the most frequently caught inshore grouper on the peninsular gulf coast. Spawning is between January and March in the offshore waters of the Continental Shelf. Juveniles inhabit nearshore and estuarine nursery areas. Though found offshore, adult gag groupers also reside in nearshore habitats.

2.4.2.4 <u>Scamp (Mycteroperca phenax)</u>. More common offshore, the adult scamp is not relatively abundant in coastal waters. Scamp spawn offshore

9

during March and April. Adults are more common over hard, broken bottoms such as rock and coral.

2.4.2.5 <u>Red snapper (Lutjanus campechanus)</u>. Although the specific spawning location is not known, red snapper probably spawn in offshore waters of the Continental Shelf from late June until October. Larvae are transported or move to coastal and estuarine waters. Juveniles prefer inshore areas of mud or sand bottoms and exercise an offshore movement as a function of size. Primarily found offshore, adult red snapper are not harvested in coastal and nearshore waters, but are an economically important species in the region.

2.4.2.6 <u>Mangrove snapper (Lutjanus griseus)</u>. Although occurring in offshore habitats, the mangrove snapper is the most common inshore snapper in the Tampa Bay study area. Adults are commonly found around structures, grassbeds, and mangroves in the estuary. However, spawning takes place offshore from April through October. Larvae are transported inshore, and juveniles are common in estuarine seagrass beds and mangrove-fringed shorelines. This species is also referred to as the gray snapper.

2.4.3 <u>Coastal Pelagic Fishes</u>

The mackerels are fast-swimming, oceanic fishes that make extensive seasonal migrations.

2.4.3.1 <u>King mackerel (Scomberomorus cavalla)</u>. The king mackerel is one of the most economically important finfish, both commercially and recreationally, in Florida. Spawning occurs in waters over the Outer Continental Shelf and in adjacent offshore currents between May and September. Little is known of juvenile forms; most inshore collections have been incidental in shrimp trawls. Adults undertake mass migrations. Evidently there are several populations of kingfish in Florida, and there is some intermixing. The gulf stock is apparently composed mostly of fish which winter between Cape Canaveral and Key West. These fish move into the gulf in the spring, move north, and spend the summer in the northern gulf as far west as Texas. A return migration to southeast Florida is demonstrated during the fall and winter. Another population of king mackerel, which is present off the southeast coast of Florida in the spring, apparently moves down the Atlantic coast to spawn. Adults feed on small schooling jacks, menhaden and other schooling herring-like fish, shrimp, and squid.

2.4.3.2 <u>Spanish mackerel (Scomberomorus maculatus)</u>. The Spanish mackerel also supports a large recreational and commercial fishery in Florida. Whereas king mackerel are not commonly associated with nearshore areas, the Spanish mackerel frequently enters saline embayments during migration. Spanish mackerel spawn over the Inner Continental Shelf from May through September. Juvenile movements are poorly known, although they are captured inshore in shrimp trawls. Separate stocks are presumed for each coast of Florida. Fish wintering in Florida Bay migrate into the northeastern gulf in the spring and return by the following winter. Spanish mackerel feed heavily on menhaden and commonly eat anchovies, small jacks, squid, and shrimp. There is a 12-inch minimum size limit imposed by the State of Florida.

10

2.5 COLONIAL BIRD NESTING SITES

Habitat diversity, mild winter climate, and geographic location allow Tampa Bay to support one of the richest assemblages of avifauna in the continental United States. The vast expanses of coastal mudflats, saline marsh, and the mangrove-sheltered embayments, as well as the marshes, wooded swamps, and cypress stands of the interior provide the forage areas and nesting substrate essential to the survival of vast populations of seabirds, shore birds, wading birds, and waterfowl which predominate in the region. Nesting colonies are depicted on the atlas by numbered symbols. Species composition of each colony is listed in Appendix D. Information pertaining to the following species was provided by the National Audubon Society, Florida Audubon Society, and Rare and Endangered Biota of Florida, Volume 2, Birds (Pritchard 1978).

2.5.1 Shore birds

Shorebirds include gulls, terns, sandpipers, plovers, stilts, skimmers, and oystercatchers. Resident nesting species use coastal mudflats, saline and brackish marshes, sheltered embayments, and estuarine and coastal open water as forage areas. Nesting usually occurs on undisturbed beaches, islands, and sand spits where vegetation is sparse of absent. Tampa Bay is host to a wide variety of migrant and wintering shore birds including plovers, sandpipers, turnstones, yellowlegs, godwits, and avocets. Gulls and terns capture small fish by hovering and diving.

2.5.1.1   American oystercatcher (Hematopus palliatus). Resident populations are estimated at between 100 and 200 pairs. This local population is augmented by winter migrants from mid-Atlantic States each year. Noncolonial nesting occurs on islands in tidal bays on unvegetated sand or shell well above the high water mark. Two or three eggs are usually laid. Oyster beds and mudflats are the primary forage areas where oystercatchers secure their diet of mollusks and crustaceans. Tampa Bay appears to be an area of concentration for this species. The American oystercatcher is listed as a species of special concern by the Florida Game and Fresh Water Fish Commission (FGFWFC).

2.5.1.2   Snowy plover (Charadrius alexandrius tenuirostris). The Cuban snowy plover is listed as an endangered species by the FGFWFC, and is currently "under review" by the U.S. Fish and Wildlife Service (USFWS). Conservative estimates place the gulf coast population at 100 pairs. Nesting habitat requirements are isolated, expansive, dry, sandy beaches where breeding takes place from April to June. Eggs, usually three, are laid in a shallow depression which is sometimes lined with shell fragments. Snowy plovers forage in search of insects, worms, mollusks, and crustaceans on dry and tidally influenced sand flats. No other bird species in Florida is so dependent on sandy beaches for nesting and foraging habitat. In general, site-specific nesting colony data are sparse for this species due to either the small numbers of individuals which constitute a colony or the transitory nature of the colony location.

2.5.1.3   Wilson's plover (Charadrius wilsonia). The Wilson's plover breeds sporadically from the Tampa Bay area southward through the Keys.

Nesting habitat diversity ranges from interior marshes to dredged spoil islands.

   2.5.1.4   Laughing gull (Larus articilla). The laughing gull is the most common breeding gull in the study area. Nests are on both natural and dredged material islands where low vegetation covers sandy soil. Typically one to three eggs are laid in late April and early May, and young birds fledge by late August. The largest laughing gull nesting colony in Florida, composed of about 20,000 individuals, was on a dredged material island in Boca Ciega Bay (Tampa Bay) until it was recently destroyed for a condominium development. The largest current colony is on dredged material disposal islands in Hillsborough Bay (Paul 1984).

   2.5.1.5   Least tern (Sterna albifrons). This easily disturbed species requires sandy, unvegetated nesting substrate such as sand spits, islands, dunes, and gravel-covered rooftops. Two eggs are usually laid in shallow scraps in the sand. Nesting begins in late April. The least tern is listed as a threatened species by the FGFWFC. It has recently been found breeding on new dredged material islands in Hillsborough Bay.

   2.5.1.6   Royal tern (Sterna maxima). This uncommon tern nests periodically in small numbers in the study area and occasionally within colonies of laughing gulls.

   2.5.1.7   Caspian tern (Sterna caspia). This uncommon tern nests on sparsely vegetated islets. The first nesting pair was found in 1961 on a dredge spoil island in Boca Ciega Bay. In 1978, 30 nesting pairs were located in Hillsborough Bay.

   2.5.1.8   Gull-billed tern (Gelochelidon nilotica). This relatively rare tern nests in low numbers with colonies of laughing gulls and black skimmers in the Tampa Bay area.

   2.5.1.9   Black skimmer (Rynchops nigra). Black skimmers nest from May through August on bare or sparsely vegetated beaches, dunes, spits, or dredged spoil islands.

2.5.2 Wading Birds

   Vast expanses of coastal and interior wetland habitat support a great number of colonial nesting wading birds including herons, egrets, and ibises. The following wading bird descriptions were taken from Palik and Lewis (1984).

   2.5.2.1   Great blue heron (Ardea herodius). The great blue heron begins nesting in early January in small numbers with other colonial waders, or in small specific colonies. Major forage areas consist of interior marshes, shallow areas of sheltered saline embayments, and inland bodies of water. Major prey are fish and crustaceans, although the diet may be augmented by small reptiles and mammals. The great blue heron is a common breeding resident in the entire study area.

2.5.2.2   Little blue heron (Florida caerulea).   The little blue heron inhabits fresh or brackish marshes.   The nesting season begins in February and lasts through August or September.   The average clutch size consists of three eggs.   Little blue herons prefer freshwater and brackish habitats in which to forage for fish, crustaceans, insects, and small reptiles and amphibians.   This species is listed by the state as a species of special concern.

2.5.2.3   Tricolored heron (Hydranassa tricolor).   The tricolored heron is common in estuarine habitats where it forages for small fish and crustaceans. Typically the breeding season extends from March to July during which time three or four eggs are laid in mixed or single species colonies.   The tricolored heron is listed as a species of special concern by the FGFWFC.

2.5.2.4   Green heron (Butorides striatus).   This common species is typically a solitary nester but will sometimes nest in small numbers on the edge of other wading bird colonies.

2.5.2.5   Black-crowned night heron (Nycticorax nycticorax).   Feeding occurs in all shallow water habitats, but breeding concentrations appear to be associated with estuarine habitats where nesting is usually in mangroves or Brazilian pepper trees (Schinus terebinthifolius).   The species breeds from March to July, and clutch size ranges from two to five eggs.   A diet composed largely of fish may be supplemented by mollusks, crustaceans, and small reptiles, amphibians, and mammals.   This is the most nocturnal foraging heron, often preying on nestlings of ibis and other herons.

2.5.2.6   Yellow-crowned night heron (Nyctanassa violacea).   More diurnal in nature than the black-crowned night heron, the yellow-crowned night heron forages on coastal mudflats for fiddler crabs and other crustaceans which constitute a major portion of the diet.   Typically forming small colonies with other yellow-crowned night herons, this bird only occasionally nests with other waders.

2.5.2.7   Cattle egret (Bubulcus ibis).   Since its first appearance in 1952, the cattle egret, an Old World species, has become the most abundant bird in mixed-species heronries in Florida.   Although it occupies coastal colonies, it rarely forages in marine and estuarine areas.

2.5.2.8   Great egret (Casmerodius albus).   The great egret uses a variety of forage habitats, from open pasture and interior impoundments to coastlines and saline marshes.   The diet consists of fish, reptiles, amphibians, birds, small mammals, and various invertebrates.   The great egret exhibits a preference for more isolated heronries, where two to six eggs are laid per clutch from March through July.

2.5.2.9   Snowy egret (Egretta thula).   Snowy egrets typically nest in mixed-species colonies.   Although widely distributed in coastal as well as interior wetlands, larger breeding colonies appear near estuarine habitats. Eggs may be laid as early as December, although most nesting is between March and August.   The snowy egret is an active predator, often running through shallow water or along the shoreline in pursuit of small fish.   The diet is

13

also supported by insects and crustaceans. The snowy egret is listed as a species of special concern by the FGFWFC.

2.5.2.10 Reddish egret (Dichromanassa rufescens). Primarily a coastal species, the reddish egret nests on mangrove islands and feeds by actively pursuing fish in the surrounding shallows. Nesting is initiated in April in Tampa Bay. Individual pairs may nest alone, or in small groups associated with mixed-species colonies. Clutch size ranges between two and five eggs. The reddish egret is listed as a species of special concern by the FGFWFC, and is currently "under review" with the USFWS.

2.3.2.11 White ibis (Eudocimus albus). This is an abundant species which flies and feeds in tight flocks. The diet consists largely of crayfish and other crustaceans, but the white ibis also eats insects, mollusks, and small fish which are secured from shallow water areas. The white ibis inhabits both freshwater and estuarine wetlands where it nests on islands, marshes, or in mangroves.

2.5.2.12 Glossy ibis (Plegadis falcinellus). This species inhabits fresh, brackish, and saltwater wetlands, nesting colonially with other wading bird species. Major foraging areas are grasslands, prairies, and high marsh areas which are exposed to seasonal inundation by rainfall. Preferred food items include crayfish and other crustaceans, and insects. Typically three or four eggs are laid in the spring with breeding continuing through the summer.

2.5.2.13 Wood stork (Mycteria americana). The wood stork inhabits freshwater and brackish marshes, where it forms large rookeries, nesting primarily in cypress swamps and protected mangrove embayments. Breeding occurs from November through January with clutch sizes ranging from two to four eggs. Primary feeding areas are pools and depressions in marshes where small fish concentrate. Feeding is accomplished by tacto-location probing. This species is listed as endangered by both the FGFWFC and the USFWS.

2.5.2.14 Anhinga (Anhinga anhinga). Although the anhinga does nest in some coastal wading bird colonies and is mapped with this group of species, it is chiefly a resident of interior and brackish wetlands. Fish constitute the bulk of the diet and are pursued and captured underwater.

2.5.2.15 Double-crested cormorant (Phalacrocorax auritus). The double-crested cormorant usually lays three or four eggs with most nesting in April through June; however, nesting has been reported throughout the year. Cormorants dive after and pursue prey underwater, returning to the surface to swallow the food item, usually fish. Double-crested cormorants nest often with colonial wading birds, and for this reason nesting sites are mapped under the heading of wading bird colonies in this atlas.

2.5.3 Eastern brown pelican (Pelecanus occidentalis carolinensis)

The eastern brown pelican is listed by FGFWFC as a species of special concern. Aerial surveys estimate the Florida breeding population to be around 8,000 pairs, of which approximately 50% are in the study area. Nesting occurs in mangroves (Rhizophora mangle, Avicennia germinans), usually on small coastal islands, from early spring through summer. Two to three eggs are usually laid, and food availability determines fledgling success. The diet consists exclusively of fish, which are secured by plunge diving. Menhaden, mullet, sardines, and pinfish are the major prey. The high incidence of first year mortality (approximately 70%) from starvation may be due to the inefficiency of the young to secure prey.

2.5.4 Other Migrant Bird Species

Other migrant species wintering throughout the study area include common loons (Gavia immer), white pelicans (Pelecanus erythrorhynchos), lesser scaups (Arythya affinis), ruddy duck (Oxyura jamaicensis), red-breasted mergansers (Mergus serrator), and roseate spoonbills (Ajaia ajaja). Migrant bird populations reach their peak between November and January.

2.6 MANATEE HABITAT

The location of all State manatee sanctuaries are shown on the individual biological resource maps and are administered by the Florida Marine Patrol, which is a branch of the Florida Department of Natural Resources. Detailed information on these sanctuaries can be found in the Boater's Guide to Manatees, the Gentle Giants (Florida Marine Patrol 1980). The manatee is considered an endangered species by both the USFWS and the FGFWFC.

2.7 SEAGRASS BEDS

Seagrass meadows have received much attention and are acknowledged to provide sediment stabilization, habitat diversity, nursery habitat for finfish and shellfish, and direct and indirect (detrital) food sources for many marine species. (Phillips 1960, 1978; Taylor and Saloman 1969; Zieman 1982; Lewis et al. 1982).

As a direct food source, seagrasses are consumed by sea urchins, a few fish species, the green turtle and the manatee (Zieman 1982). As habitat, seagrass meadows are particularly important as nursery grounds for juveniles of pink shrimp, several species of grunts and snappers, snook, spotted seatrout, red drum, and sheepshead. The adult form of some of these species may be more commonly associated with other habitats (such as the association of snook with mangroves), but the seagrass nursery habitat is probably vital in providing for adults to be available to commercial and recreational fisheries.

Lewis et al. (1984) reported the occurrence of five species of seagrasses in Tampa Bay:

1. Thalassia testudinum (turtlegrass)
2. Halodule wrightii (shoalgrass)
3. Syringodium filiforme (manateegrass)
4. Ruppia maritima (widgeongrass)
5. Halophila engelmannii

15

Lewis et al. (1984) estimates that there are 14,202 acres of seagrass in Tampa Bay.

Seagrass beds are portrayed by a habitat screen on the individual biological resource maps. They were delineated from seagrass maps from Lewis (1980) and from 1982 color photography, at a 1:24,000 scale.

2.8 MACROALGAE

Several hundred macroalgae species are found within the Tampa Bay study region (Humm 1973). Macroalgae are frequently the most conspicuous flora in shallow water and proliferate below depths tolerated by seagrasses.

The Tampa Bay study area is the boundary area between tropical and temperate species of brown algae (McNulty et al. 1972). Fifty-one percent of the macroalgae found in the study area are red algae (Rhodophyta), 18% are brown algae (Phaeophyta), and 31% are green algae (Chlorophyta) (Humm 1973).

Unfortunately, the faunal assemblages associated with algal communities in the study area and their ecological roles as habitat and food sources are almost entirely unknown (Palik and Lewis 1984).

During macroalgae blooms, the algae compete with seagrasses for light. These blooms are caused by eutrophication in Tampa Bay.

Macroalgae beds are not mapped on the atlas.

2.9 ARTIFICIAL REEFS

The artificial reefs program of the State of Florida is administered by the Bureau of Marine Science and Technology under Section 370.013 of the Florida Statutes. Approximately $110,000 in grants were awarded in 1979 and 1980, which were the first 2 years of the newly adopted program (Florida Department of Natural Resources 1981). The principal types of fish inhabiting artificial reefs in the study area's coastal waters are grouper, snapper, Spanish mackerel, king mackerel, and amberjack. A list of artificial reefs keyed by number on the atlas overlays is shown in Table 1.

Florida's coastal waters contain more artificial reefs than any other state (Seaman 1982). Scientific development and deployment of artificial reefs have been slow, with little research and little funding. Without considerable volunteer effort to secure materials and free labor, many of the present artificial reefs in the Tampa Bay study area would not exist. The largest group of organizations which have put together an artificial reef program is in Pinellas County. The cities of Clearwater, Madeira Beach, St. Petersburg, St. Petersburg Beach, and Treasure Island and the Pinellas County Board of Commissioners have built 20 reefs, 10 of which are presently maintained by Pinellas County Mosquito Control. Its annual budget supports a small crew, barge rental, operating expenses, and equipment (Seaman 1982).

16

Table 1. Artificial reefs.

Number on map	Composition	Latitude	Longitude	Depth (ft)	Distance offshore (mi)
1	Concrete rubble, 32-ft steel hull ships	27°47'11"	82°35'37"	34-36	1.0
2	Tires, metal junk, concrete rubble	27°47'06"	82°50'02"	20-22	1.0
3	Tires, metal junk, concrete rubble	27°47'00"	82°49'08"	20-22	1.3
4	Tires, clay pipes, concrete rubble	27°46'32"	82°35'48"	16	1.3
5	Tires, clay pipes, concrete rubble	27°40'56"	82°38'01"	11	1.3
6	Autos	27°39'17"	82°35'28"	25	2.1
7	Concrete pipe	27°36'00"	82°46'00"	9	0.4
8	Concrete, tires	27°31'42"	82°38'42"	15	0.1
9	Concrete, tires	27°30'24"	82°35'00"	12	0.1
10	Tires, broken concrete, sewer tile	27°23'51"	82°35'49"	12	1.0

Virtually all artificial reefs in Florida are composed of either ships, automobiles, tires, or concrete. New prefabricated artificial reefs are being introduced in Florida (off Fort Lauderdale, Panama City, and Jacksonville) by the Japanese under contract with the National Marine Fisheries Service.

3. WATER RESOURCES

3.1 SALINITY

Salinities have been routinely measured in Tampa Bay since 1954. Since Tampa Bay is a stream-fed estuary, salinities are lowest at the time of maximum stream discharge (normally during the late summer and early fall) and highest at the time of minimum stream discharge (early winter). Historical salinities have ranged from 0.9 to 30.3 parts per thousand (ppt) in Old Tampa Bay (23.5 ppt mean), from 7.4 to 31.9 ppt in Hillsborough Bay (21.8 ppt mean), from 14.0 to 36.8 ppt in Tampa Bay (28.4 ppt mean), from 22.7 to 37.3 ppt in Boca Ciega Bay (32.6 ppt mean), from 1.0 to 33.7 ppt in the lower Manatee River (24.5 ppt mean), and 33.9 to 36.4 ppt in Sarasota Bay (35.4 ppt mean). These salinities are based on observations from 1954 to 1965 by Carl Saloman (McNulty et al. 1972).

Specific conductivity has been measured in Tampa Bay since 1972 by the Hillsborough County Environmental Protection Commission (HCEPC). Salinity is still measured, but the continuity of its data record is not as good as the conductivity data. Specific conductivity or "electrical conductance" is a measure of the ability of water to conduct an electrical current. It is defined as the reciprocal of the resistance in ohms measured between opposite faces of a centimeter cube of an aqueous solution and is expressed in micromhos per centimeter (μmhos/cm) (Slack and Kaufman 1973).

The relationship of salinity to specific conductivity is well defined, and salinity can be estimated accurately from conductivity data alone. The 1981 mean salinity for all 81 HCEPC water quality stations was 20.5 ppt; average conductivity was 32,200 μmhos/cm. To convert conductivity (μmhos/cm) to salinity (ppt), divide the conductivity data by 1,570.

3.2 POINT SOURCE DISCHARGES

3.2.1 Industrial Point Source Discharges

The Florida Department of Environmental Regulation (FDER) in Tallahassee keeps an updated computer data base on all industrial point source discharges in the study area. Individual point source discharges are numbered and plotted on the individual atlas maps. A list describing each individual point source is found in Table 2 (Florida Department of Environmental Regulation 1983a).

18

Table 2. Industrial point source discharges (Florida Department of Environmental Regulation 1983a).

Number on map	Name	Latitude	Longitude	Owner-ship	Receiving body	Capacity	County	Process or treatment
1	Amoco oil separator	27°56'00"	82°27'00"	Private	Sparkman Channel	N/A[a]	Hills.	Evap. perc. lagoon
2	Chevron USA 1,2,3	27°57'30"	82°32'30"	Private	Tampa Bay	N/A	Hills.	Unknown
3	Del Monte Corp.	27°57'30"	82°25'30"	Private	Drainage ditch	N/A	Hills.	Surface drainage
4	Fleet Transport Co.	27°56'27"	82°26'26"	Private	McKay Bay	80TGD	Hills.	Tank truck wash
5	Gardinier, Inc.	27°51'38"	82°23'27"	Private	Alafia River	N/A	Hills.	Unknown
6	Gibsonton Speedwash	27°51'13"	82°22'59"	Private	Hillsborough Bay	N/A	Hills.	Trickling filter, chlorination
7	IMC Port Sutton #1	27°54'10"	82°24'26"	Private	Port Sutton Canal	864TGD	Hills.	IMC - Port Sutton
8	Nitram Chemical #1	27°54'40"	82°23'50"	Private	Delaney Creek	N/A	Hills.	Unknown
9	Ruskin Laundromat	27°43'13"	82°25'58"	Private	Little Manatee Rd.	10TGD	Hills.	Trickling filter
10	Seaboard Coastline RR	27°57'21"	82°23'44"	Private	Palm River	N/A	Hills.	Unknown
11	TECO Big Bend coal runoff	27°47'42"	82°24'16"	Private	Tampa Bay	33MGD	Hills.	Unknown

(continued)

19

Table 2 (continued)

Number on map	Name	Latitude	Longitude	Owner-ship	Receiving body	Capacity	County	Process or treatment
12	TECO Big Bend cooling water	27°47'36"	82°24'10"	Private	Hillsborough Bay	N/A	Hills.	Unknown
13	TECO Big Bend slag pond	27°47'37"	82°24'35"	Private	Hillsborough Bay	N/A	Hills.	Unknown
14	TECO Gannon discharge	27°54'21"	82°25'21"	Private	Hillsborough Bay	1268MGD	Hills.	Unknown
15	TECO Gannon saltwater pond	27°54'28"	82°25'24"	Private	Hillsborough Bay	N/A	Hills.	Unknown
16	TECO Hookers Point	27°56'18"	82°26'35"	Private	Sparkman Channel	N/A	Hills.	Unknown
17	TECO Hookers Point outfall	27°56'11"	82°26'35"	Private	Sparkman Channel	N/A	Hills.	Unknown
18	W.R. Grace NH3 terminal	27°54'10"	82°25'30"	Private	Port Sutton Canal	N/A	Hills.	Unknown
19	AMAX Piney Point	27°37'39"	82°31'21"	Private	Bishop Harbor	N/A	Manatee	Unknown
20	AMAX Piney Point	27°37'39"	82°31'21"	Private	Bishop Harbor	N/A	Manatee	Unknown
21	AMAX Piney Point	27°37'39"	82°31'21"	Private	Piney Point	N/A	Manatee	Unknown

(continued)

20

Table 2 (continued)

Number on map	Name	Latitude	Longitude	Owner-ship	Receiving body	Capacity	County	Process or treatment
22	Beker Rock terminal	27°35'59"	82°33'47"	Private	Tampa Bay	N/A	Manatee	Unknown
23	Nord Southern	27°30'50"	82°33'20"	Private	Manatee River	N/A	Manatee	Unknown
24	Dixie Plating, Inc	27°48'48"	82°40'32"	Private	Joe's Creek	N/A	Pinellas	Unknown
25	Florida Power Bartow discharge	27°51'40"	82°36'09"	Private	Tampa Bay	N/A	Pinellas	Cooling water collection & storage
26	Florida Power Higgins discharge	28°00'04"	82°39'45"	Private	Tampa Bay	N/A	Pinellas	Cooling water discharge
27	Modern Plating Corp.	27°52'15"	83°42'15"	Private	Cross Bayou Canal	N/A	Pinellas	Rinse water discharge
28	PBC Industries	27°49'00"	82°41'30"	Private	Joe's Creek	N/A	Pinellas	Unknown
29	Pinellas Industries	27°54'03"	82°46'09"	Private	Gulf of Mexico	N/A	Pinellas	Unknown
30	Sand Key Condos	27°56'40"	82°50'08"	Private	Clearwater Harbor	N/A	Pinellas	Unknown
31	MRI Corporation	27°52'36"	82°21'18"	Private	Six Mile Creek	N/A	Hills.	Unknown

(continued)

21

Table 2 (concluded)

Number on map	Name	Latitude	Longitude	Owner-ship	Receiving body	Capacity	County	Process or treatment
32	Trademark Nitrogen	27°57'14"	82°20'58"	Private	Six Mile Creek	300TGO	Hills.	Unknown
33	Belcher oil/water separator	27°38'19"	82°33'28"	Private	Tampa Bay	N/A	Manatee	Unknown
34	Amcon Concrete, Inc.	(56th St., north of Hills Ave.)		Private	Ditch	N/A	Hills.	Unknown
35	Shell Oil Co.	(Port of Tampa)		Private	Tampa Bay	N/A	Hills.	Oil/water separation
36	Beker Plant outfall	27°30'00"	82°38'20"	Private	Wingate Creek	N/A	Manatee	Unknown
37	Tropicana	27°31'05"	82°32'00"	Private	Robinson's Ditch	N/A	Manatee	Aeration & sprayfield
38	Tropicana	27°31'05"	82°32'00"	Private	Manatee River	N/A	Manatee	Aeration & sprayfield

a N/A = Not available.

22

3.2.2 Municipal Point Sources Discharges

The FDER keeps an updated computer data base on all industrial point source discharges in the study area. Individual municipal point source discharges are numbered and plotted on the individual atlas maps. A list describing each individual point source is found in Table 3 (Florida Department of Environmental Regulation 1983b).

3.2.3 Municipal Point Source Discharges Processing Hazardous Wastes

All municipal point source discharges located in the study area process hazardous waste according to Moon (personal communication 1984). Hazardous waste includes any toxic substance which could poison the environment if not disposed of properly. Examples include petroleum products, pesticides, herbicides, nuclear wastes, and most chemicals.

3.3 DREDGE SPOIL DISPOSAL AREAS

The U.S. Army Corps of Engineers is the Federal agency responsible for all dredge and fill activity in the State. A permit must be obtained from the Corps before any dredge and fill activity will be allowed. The FDER is the State agency responsible for permitting all dredge spoil disposal sites in the State. They maintain location maps and site data on all dredge spoil disposal sites in the study area. Individual public or private dredge spoil sites have been plotted on the atlas overlays and represent all dredge spoil disposal sites permitted by the FDER.

3.4 TIDE STATIONS

3.4.1 Tide Station Locations

The National Ocean Service (NOS) has collected tidal data at 104 station locations in the study area. The Clearwater and St. Petersburg Municpal Pier tide stations are the only permanent NOS tide stations in the study area. Individual sites at which data have been collected are numbered and plotted on the individual atlas overlays. Table 4 describes the station and its data record (NOS 1983). Tidal data may be ordered from these stations from the following address:

Tidal Acquisition
National Ocean Service
6001 Executive Boulevard
Rockville, MD 20852
Attn: N/OMS 121.

3.4.2 Tidal Datums

The latest tidal datums for the permanent NOS tide stations located in Clearwater and St. Petersburg are listed in Table 5.

23

Table 3. Municipal point source discharges (Florida Department of Environmental Regulations 1983b).

Number on map	Name	Latitude	Longitude	Owner-ship	Receiving body	Capacity[a]	County	Process or treatment
1	Apollo Beach	27°45'50"	82°24'31"	County	Tampa Bay	1.0MGD	Hills.	Extended aeration
2	Bahia Beach	27°43'45"	82°28'30"	Private	Tampa Bay	100TGD	Hills.	Extended aeration
3	Bayshore Palms Apts.	27°52'00"	82°29'22"	Municipal	Hillsborough Bay	10TGD	Hills.	Extended aeration
4	City of Palmetto	27°31'40"	82°35'40"	Municipal	Terra Ceia Bay	1.4MGD	Manatee	Expanded Bardenpho process
5	Tidevue Estates	27°31'33"	82°31'47"	County	Drainage ditch	100TGD	Manatee	AWT
6	Aerosonics Corp.	27°58'54"	82°45'20"	Private	Alligator Creek	7.5TGD	Pinellas	Extended aeration
7	Town of Belleair	27°56'04"	82°48'03"	Municipal	Clearwater Harbor	900TGD	Pinellas	Activated sludge & tertiary
8	Boulevard TP	27°57'45"	82°44'38"	Private	Tampa Bay	16.5TGD	Pinellas	Extended aeration
9	Clearwater - East	27°57'32"	82°42'28"	Municipal	Tampa Bay	5.0MGD	Pinellas	Activated sludge
10	Clearwater - Marshall St.	27°58'50"	82°47'13"	Municipal	Stevenson's Creek	10.0MGD	Pinellas	Activated sludge
11	Clearwater - NE	28°01'15"	82°42'00"	Municipal	Tampa Bay	8.0MGD	Pinellas	Contact stabilization
12	Dyna-Flo Services	28°02'05"	82°44'25"	Private	Curlew Creek	1.0MGD	Pinellas	Extended aeration

(continued)

24

Table 3 (continued)

Number on map	Name	Latitude	Longitude	Owner-ship	Receiving body	Capacity[a]	County	Process or treatment
13	Ft. DeSoto Park #1	(North beach)		County	Tampa Bay	30TGD	Pinellas	Extended aeration
14	Ft. DeSoto Park #2	(Fort area)		County	Tampa Bay	12TGD	Pinellas	Extended aeration
15	Ft. DeSota Park #3	(East area)		County	Tampa Bay	12TGD	Pinellas	Extended aeration
16	Ft. DeSota Park #4	(Camping area)		County	Tampa Bay	80TGD	Pinellas	Extended aeration
17	Town of Indian Shores	27°50'50"	82°50'53"	Municipal	The Narrows	750TGD	Pinellas	Activated sludge
18	Kakusha MHP	27°56'08"	82°47'56"	Private	Clearwater Harbor	16.6TGD	Pinellas	Extended aeration
19	City of Largo	27°54'28"	82°42'16"	Municipal	Feather Sound	15.0MGD	Pinellas	Unknown
20	McKay Creek	27°52'40"	82°51'00"	County	Boca Ciega Bay	6.0MGD	Pinellas	Activated sludge
21	City of Oldsmar	28°01'40"	82°39'30"	Municipal	Mobbly Bay	1.0MGD	Pinellas	Extended aeration
22	Ranch Mobile	27°54'22"	82°43'56"	Private	Long Branch	150TGD	Pinellas	Trickling filter
23	South Cross Bayou	27°49'38"	82°44'30"	County	Joe's Creek	28.5MGD	Pinellas	Contact stabilization
24	South Gate Park	27°57'13"	82°43'55"	Private	Tampa Bay	50.0TGD	Pinellas	Trickling filter
25	Southern Comfort TP	27°59'20"	82°43'40"	Private	Tampa Bay	6.0TGD	Pinellas	Extended aeration
26	City of St. Pete - Albert Whitted	27°45'52"	82°37'39"	Municipal	Tampa Bay	20.0MGD	Pinellas	Contact stabilization

(continued)

25

Table 3 (concluded)

Number on map	Name	Latitude	Longitude	Owner-ship	Receiving body	Capacity[a]	County	Process or treatment
27	City of St. Pete-NW	27°47'40"	82°44'30"	Municipal	Boca Ciega Bay	20.0MGD	Pinellas	Activated sludge
28	City of St. Pete-SW	27°43'05"	82°41'09"	Municipal	Tampa Bay	20.0MGD	Pinellas	Tertiary
29	City of St. Pete-NE	(62nd Ave. & 16th St. NE)		Municipal	Tampa Bay	16.0MGD	Pinellas	Activated sludge
30	Eastside Water Co	27°59'16"	82°22'27"	Private	Harney Canal	250TGD	Hills.	Trickling filter
31	Progress Village	27°52'36"	82°22'18"	Private	Archie's Creek	260TGD	Hills.	Activated sludge
32	River Oaks	28°01'37"	82°34'55"	County	Rocky Creek	4.6MGD	Hills.	Advanced waste treatment
33	City of Bradenton	27°27'32"	82°32'36"	Municipal	Manatee River	6.0MGD	Manatee	Contact stabilization
34	Tillman Elementary School	(Palmetto)		County	Manatee River	10TGD	Manatee	Extended aeration
35	Dolomite Utilities	27°23'30"	82°32'25"	Private	Whitaker Bayou	450TGD	Sarasota	Rotating biological contact
36	City of Tampa	(Hookers Point)		Municipal	Hillsborough Bay	55MGD	Hills.	Tertiary

a MGD = million gal/day.
 TGD = thousand gal/day.

26

Table 4. National Ocean Service (NOS) tide station data (NOS 1983).

Number on map	NOS I.D.	Station name	Latitude	Longitude	Date installed	Date removed
1	2726247	Bradenton, Manatee River	27°30.0'	82°34.4'	10/06/75	04/23/79
2	8726249	Palma Sola Bay North	27°30.2'	82°38.9'	03/30/77	11/04/77
3	8726273	De Soto Point	27°31.4'	82°39.0'	03/30/77	10/27/77
4	8726282	Anna Maria	27°32.0'	82°43.8'	03/24/76	10/04/76
5	8726311	Belville Point	27°33.8'	82°35.2'	03/28/77	10/25/77
6	8726318	Boots Point	27°34.1'	82°35.8'	03/28/77	10/25/77
7	8726319	Seabreeze Point	27°34.2'	82°34.2	03/28/77	10/25/77
8	8726347	Egmont Key	27°36.0'	82°45.6'	07/20/76	11/04/76
9	8726348	Two Bros. Island	27°35.8'	82°35.0'	04/07/77	04/19/79
10	8726353	Bishop Harbor	27°36.1'	82°33.2'	03/23/77	11/09/77
11	8726364	Mullet Key	27°36.9'	82°43.6'	03/24/76	04/06/77
12	8726367	Mullet Key Bayou	27°37.3'	82°43.6'	07/21/76	12/10/76
13	8726384	Port Manatee	27°38.1'	82°33.6'	03/24/76	12/05/77
14	8726385	Mullet Key Bayou	27°38.8'	82°43.0'	06/03/76	11/04/76
15	8726425	Cockroach Bay	27°40.9'	82°30.2'	04/19/77	04/18/79
16	8726428	Tierra Verde	27°41.3'	82°43.0'	06/22/76	11/04/76
17	8726430	St. Peterburg Beach	27°41.0'	82°44.3'	06/24/76	11/01/76
18	8726436	Little Manatee River	27°42.3'	82°26.9'	01/13/77	04/25/79
19	8726437	Big Cockroach Mound	27°41.2'	82°31.3'	05/19/76	08/18/76
20	8726441	Pass-A-Grille Ch.East	27°41.5'	82°43.8'	03/24/76	10/12/76
21	8726442	Pass-A-Grille Ch., B.C.B.	27°41.4'	82°44.2'	10/13/49	08/18/52
22	8726454	Point Pinellas	27°42.1'	82°38.4'	09/24/75	04/07/77
23	8726467	Marsh Branch, Ruskin	27°43.1'	82°27.2'	01/13/77	05/03/77
24	8726468	Shell Point	27°43.1'	82°28.8'	01/12/77	05/03/77
25	8726474	Little Bayou	27°43.6'	82°38.1'	08/19/76	01/04/77
26	8726479	Bahia Beach	27°43.8'	82°28.6'	01/13/77	05/04/77
27	8726485	Big Bayou	27°44.1'	82°38.3'	08/19/76	01/04/77
28	8726486	Gulfport	27°44.2'	82°42.4'	10/08/75	07/08/77
29	8726492	Mangrove Point	27°44.5'	82°28.0'	03/14/77	10/26/77
30	8726494	Long Key	27°45.1'	82°45.1'	06/04/76	11/05/76
31	8726505	Treasure Island	27°45.4'	82°45.6'	05/14/76	11/10/76
32	8726520	St. Petersburg	27°46.4'	82°37.3'	12/14/46	In Operation
33	8720521	St. Petersburg (B)	27°46.4'	82°37.3'	10/01/76	In Operation
34	8726533	Johns Pass	27°47.1'	82°49.9'	05/14/76	08/06/76
35	8726537	Apollo Beach	27°47.2'	82°25.6'	03/24/76	02/01/78
36	8726538	Jungle Estates	27°47.3'	82°45.3'	06/01/76	09/24/76
37	8726539	Newman Branch	27°47.0'	82°24.4'	03/08/77	10/08/77
38	8726557	Welch Causeway	27°48.4'	82°47.7'	08/01/51	01/30/52
39	8726562	Hillsborough Bay E.	27°48.4'	27°24.7'	03/09/77	10/06/77
40	8726568	Bay Pines, Long Bayou	27°48.9'	82°45.9'	06/01/76	09/24/76
41	8726571	Mermaid Point	27°49.2'	82°35.5'	08/18/76	01/04/77

(continued)

27

Table 4.   (continued)

Number on map	NOS I.D.	Station name	Latitude	Longitude	Date installed	Date removed
42	8726572	The Kitchen	27°49.2'	82°23.2'	03/07/77	04/18/79
43	8726573	Gadsden Point	27°49.3'	82°29.1'	11/05/75	01/06/76
44	8726574	Boca Ciega Bay	27°48.5'	82°47.7'	06/30/76	09/24/76
45	8726581	Sand Key	27°50.2'	82°50.2'	03/25/76	08/10/76
46	8726587	Bullfrog Creek	27°50.2'	82°23.2'	01/12/77	05/03/77
47	8726588	Long Bayou North	27°50.1'	82°46.4'	06/01/76	09/24/76
48	8726589	Cross Bayou South	27°50.1	82°45.2	07/14/76	11/03/76
49	8726594	Bayou Grande North	27°50.6'	82°36.6'	08/17/76	01/07/77
50	8726601	Indian Rocks Beach	27°52.4	82°51.1'	11/25/72	01/06/73
51	8726602	Gibsonton	27°50.6'	82°23.7'	03/17/77	11/02/77
52	8726603	Rivera Bay	27°51.2'	82°37.3'	08/17/76	01/07/77
53	8726604	Long Shoal	27°51.3'	82°28.8'	11/05/75	01/06/76
54	8726605	Tinney Creek	27°51.1'	82°37.9'	08/18/76	01/18/77
55	8726606	The Narrows	27°51.5'	82°50.7'	03/25/76	07/17/76
56	8726609	Alafia River	27°51.6'	82°23.0'	12/07/76	05/02/77
57	8726612	Shug Harbor	27°51.7'	82°37.2'	08/17/76	03/02/77
58	8726621	Port Tampa	27°52.0'	82°23.3'	09/17/76	02/09/77
59	8726623	Indian Rocks Pier	27°53.7'	82°51.1'	04/27/76	11/09/76
60	8726625	Indian Rocks Beach	27°52.6'	82°51.0'	03/25/76	09/08/76
61	8726632	Archie Creek	27°52.9'	82°23.8'	12/09/76	05/02/77
62	8726639	Tampa, Ballast Point	27°53.4'	82°28.8'	10/30/75	04/25/79
63	8726641	Gandy Bridge	27°53.6'	82°32.3'	10/01/75	07/07/77
64	8726643	Anona	27°53.2'	82°50.4'	03/30/76	08/09/76
65	8726648	Frankland Bridge	27°53.7'	82°38.3'	08/25/76	01/06/77
66	8726651	Pendola Point	27°54.0'	82°25.4'	02/23/77	08/03/77
67	8726657	Dan's Island	27°54.5'	82°27.1'	11/30/76	04/07/77
68	8726661	Tampa, Knight AP	27°27.0'	82°27.0'	01/22/47	03/24/48
69	8726662	Cross Bayou Canal	27°54.8'	82°41.9'	10/22/75	01/09/76
70	8726666	Belleair	27°55.1'	82°49.6'	03.25/76	08/09/76
71	8726667	McKay Bay	27°54.9'	82°25.4'	03/24/76	04/07/77
72	8726668	Tampa, Hookers Pt.	27°55.1'	82°26.7'	11/30/76	04/16/79
73	8726685	22 St. Causeway	27°56.3'	82°25.9'	01/14/77	01/18/78
74	8726686	Belleair Beach	27°56.1'	82°50.4'	03/25/76	06/29/76
75	8726687	Allen Creek	27°56.2'	82°43.8'	08/26/76	01/11/77
76	8726688	Seddon Island	27°56.0'	82°26.8'	11/30/76	03/29/79
77	8726689	Bay Arist. Village	27°56.5'	82°43.2'	10/30/75	07/06/77
78	8726692	Tampa, Seddon Is.	27°56.4'	82°27.0'	04/01/26	06/30/26
79	8726693	Hills. River Inlet	27°56.8'	82°27.7'	10/29/76	03/03/77
80	8726696	Palm River Ent.	27°56.8'	82°24.1'	12/06/76	04/06/77
81	8726699	Palm River, FL	27°56.9'	82°23.1'	12/06/76	04/06/77
82	8726706	Clearwater	27°57.3'	82°48.4'	10/07/75	12/06/77
83	8726707	Bayview	27°57.4'	82°42.7'	03/18/58	05/26/58
84	8726711	West Tampa	27°57.6'	82°28.1'	10/29/76	02/09/77

(continued)

Table 4.   (concluded)

Number on map	NOS I.D.	Station name	Latitude	Longitude	Date installed	Date removed
85	8726714	Rocky Point	27°57.9'	82°33.9'	10/15/76	03/03/77
86	8726721	Courtney Campbell	27°58.2'	82°37.5'	06/09/47	09/17/47
87	8726724	Clearwater Beach	27°58.6'	82°49.9'	04/19/73	01/12/81
88	8726725	Clearwater Bay	27°58.5'	82°48.1'	10/16/75	12/10/75
89	8726726	Clearwater Beach (B)	27°58.6'	82°49.9'	10/01/76	In Operation
90	8726727	Sweet Water Creek	27°58.7'	82°33.7'	09/28/76	03/02/77
91	8726737	Rocky Creek Ent.	27°59.3'	82°35.8'	11/18/76	05/02/77
92	8726738	Safety Harbor	27°59.3'	82°41.1'	12/19/75	12/06/77
93	8726739	Dick Creek	27°59.3'	82°36.5'	02/10/77	08/01/77
94	8726748	Rocky Creek	27°59.8'	82°35.3'	09/27/76	04/05/77
95	8726768	Double Branch	28°01.7'	82°38.0'	09/30/76	02/08/77
96	8726769	Mobbly Bayou	28°01.3'	82°39.3'	10/18/76	04/18/77
97	8726778	Oldsmar	28°02.1'	82°40.7'	09/28/76	02/08/77
98	8726789	Possum Branch	28°02.3'	82°41.9'	11/11/76	04/05/77
99	8726759	Double Branch Bay	28°00.3'	82°37.2'	02/08/77	08/01/77
100	8726614	Alafia River North	27°52.2'	82°19.7'	12/09/76	05/02/77
101	8726278	Redfish Point	27°31.6'	82°28.9'	03/24/77	10/20/77
102	8726277	Fort Hamer	27°31.5'	82°25.8'	03/24/77	04/16/79
103	8726238	Braden Point	27°29.2'	82°30.3'	04/04/77	10/26/77
104	8726159	Whitfield Estates	27°24.5'	82°34.8'	04/25/77	11/09/77

Table 5.   National Ocean Service (NOS) 1983 tidal datums for the NOS Clearwater and St. Petersburg, Florida, tide stations (NOS personal communication 1984).

Parameter	Clearwater	St. Petersburg
Mean higher high water	2.10 ft.	2.24 ft
Mean high water	1.80 ft	1.96 ft
Mean tide level	0.90 ft.	1.17 ft
Mean low water	0.00 ft	0.39 ft
Mean lower low water	-0.50 ft	0.00 ft

3.5 WATER QUALITY

The Hillsborough County Environmental Protection Commission has collected monthly water quality data from approximately 81 sampling stations in the study area since 1972. The data from these stations were used exclusively to generate the 5-year seasonally averaged water quality parameter means presented in this atlas.

Most of the problems with water quality in Tampa Bay are found in Hillsborough Bay where high fecal coliform, phosphorus, chlorophyll, turbidity, and low dissolved oxygen persist. The north prong of the Alafia River exhibits the worst water quality problem found in the Alafia River Basin. High nutrient levels, as well as low dissolved oxygen, can probably be attributed to phosphate mining activities in this watershed. The Little Manatee River has high phosphorus and fecal coliform levels which probably result from agricultural and rangeland activities in the region. The Manatee River exhibits no major water quality problems.

3.5.1 Methodology

For the purposes of this study, the following five water quality parameters have been seasonally averaged for the most recent 5-year data period available (September 1978 through August 1983):

1. Total chlorophyll (µg/l)
2. Specific conductivity (middepth; µmhos/cm)
3. Turbidity (NTU)
4. Temperature (middepth; °C)
5. Total nitrogen (mg/l)

The locations of all the sampling stations averaged by season for this study are numbered and plotted on the individual atlas maps. The seasonal averages by water quality parameter for each station are listed in Appendix A and are listed by station on the supplemental map legend. For purposes of this study, winter is composed of the months of December, January, and February; spring is March, April, and May; summer is June, July, and August and fall is September, October, and November.

3.5.2 Total Chlorophyll

Total chlorophyll is an indirect measure of the quantity of planktonic algae present in a body of water and as such is an indicator of eutrophication. It is measured in micro-grams per liter (µg/l). Total chlorophyll varies seasonally and is highest in the summer and lowest in the winter.

A complete isopleth map of the 5-year annual mean for total chlorophyll is shown in Figure 3. Most of the water quality problems associated with high total chlorophyll levels are in Hillsborough Bay. A lesser area of high chlorophyll levels is in extreme western Old Tampa Bay. High chlorophyll levels are associated with algal blooms. One type of algae, the dinoflagellate species, _Ptychodiscus brevis_, is a toxic red-tide organism which has plagued Tampa Bay for many years. In 1971, Tampa Bay experienced a major red-tide

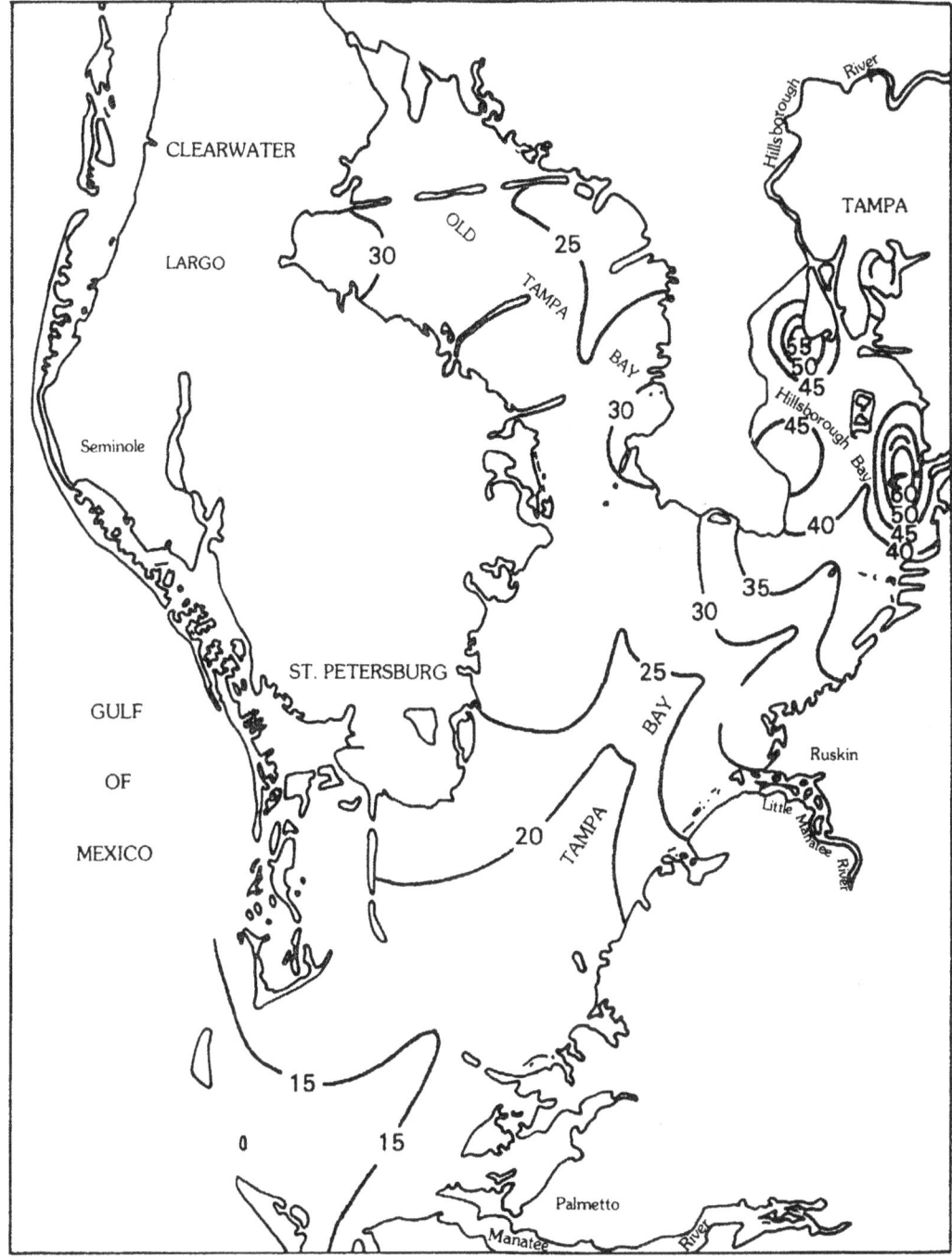

Figure 3. Isopleth map of mean annual total chlorophyll (μg/l) for Tampa Bay; 5-year mean, Sept. 1978 - Aug. 1983 (data from Hillsborough County Environmental Protection Commission 1983).

outbreak which was responsible for the death of millions of fish throughout the bay. Another lesser outbreak was in 1974. Minor outbreaks were in 1978, 1979, 1980, 1981, and 1983 with no significant fish kills (Wilkins 1983).

3.5.3 Specific Conductivity

Specific conductivity is a measure of the ability of water to conduct an electrical current. It is measured in micromhos per centimeter (μmhos/cm) at standard temperature (25 °C) and pressure (760 mm/Hg) (Slack and Kaufman 1973). Specific conductivity is easily determined by a field meter, and it is a good indicator of salinity.

Specific conductivity levels vary seasonally and correlate well with stream discharge. During the late summer and early fall, when stream discharge normally is at its annual maximum, conductivity levels normally reach their annual minimum as freshwater discharge mixes with bay waters. During the early winter when stream discharge usually reaches its annual minimum conductivity levels are normally at their highest annual levels (see Figure 4). Minimum bay conductivity levels are always at times of maximum streamflow. Maximum conductivity levels are at the end of sustained low-flow periods. Maximum and minimum conductivity levels are usually about two months apart.

Conductivity levels are lowest in the upper reaches of Tampa Bay nearest the freshwater discharge sources and progressively increase, reaching their greatest levels near the mouth of Tampa Bay (see Figure 5).

Conductivity values on the maps are in mmhos/cm. The values in the supplemental legend should be in μmhos/cm and are mislabeled on the maps. To convert conductivity (mmhos/cm) to salinity (ppt), divide the conductivity data by 1.57.

3.5.4 Turbidity

Turbidity is an expression of the optical quality of a water sample to scatter and absorb light rather than transmit light in straight lines. It is measured in Nephelometric Turbidity Units (NTU's). High turbidity levels are not always associated with poor water quality. Rather, they reflect the material held in suspension in the water column. High-turbidity levels may be associated with algal blooms, dredging activities, or with suspended solids associated with high wind-driven waves in shallow areas of the bay.

The highest turbidity levels found in Tampa Bay are located in Hillsborough Bay, extreme western Old Tampa Bay, and at the mouth of the Little Manatee River. These three areas all exhibit moderate to heavy algal blooms primarily during the spring months. In Tampa Bay as a whole, turbidity varies seasonally, reaching a peak in the spring and its lowest point during the winter. A complete isopleth map of mean annual turbidity levels for Tampa Bay for the past 5 years is shown is Figure 6.

3.5.5 Temperature

Water temperature is cyclic in Tampa Bay and is measured in either degrees

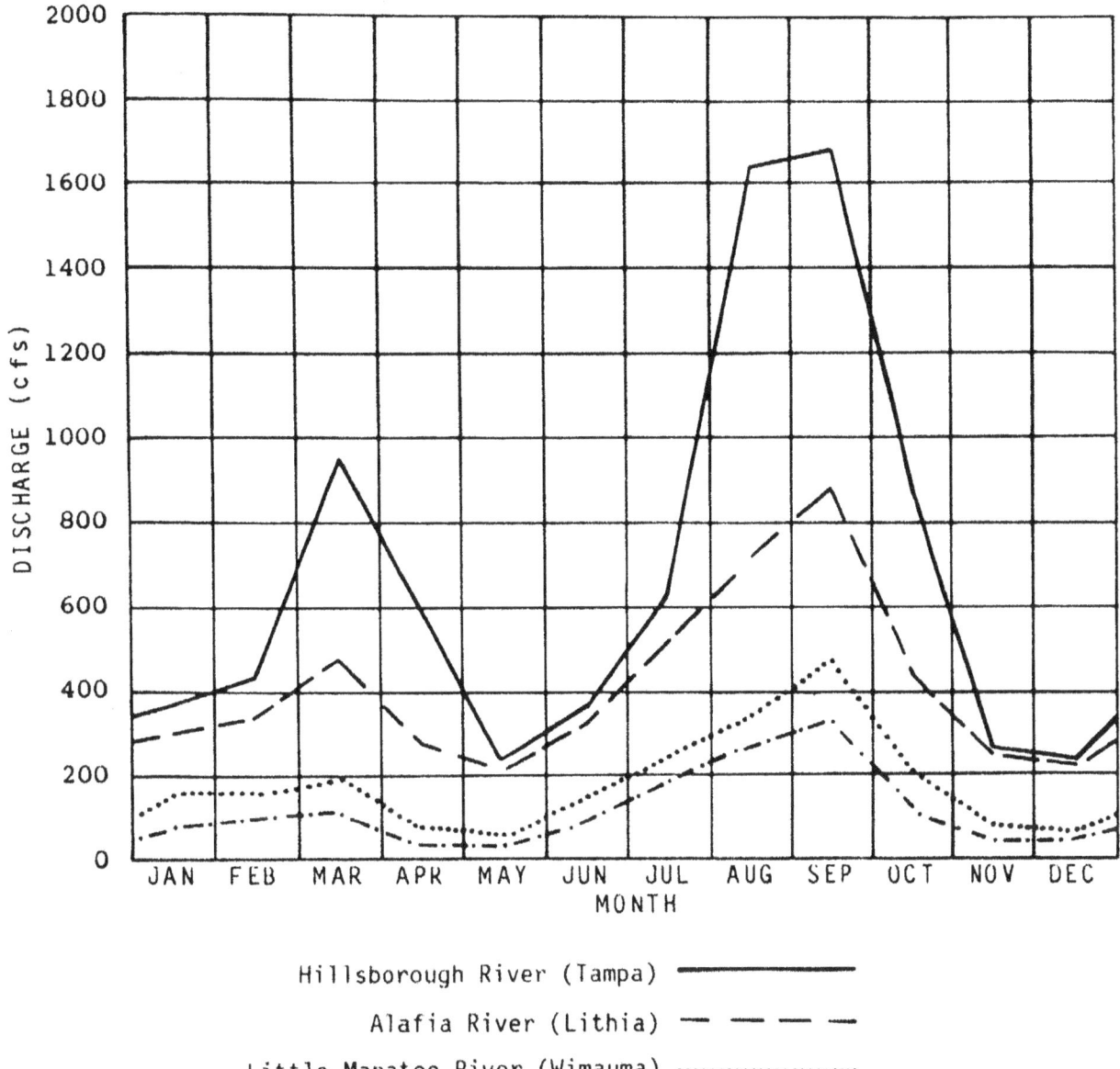

Figure 4. Mean monthly stream discharge (1952-1966) for four major rivers discharging into Tampa Bay; 5-year mean, Sept. 1978 - Aug. 1983 (data from McNulty et al. 1972).

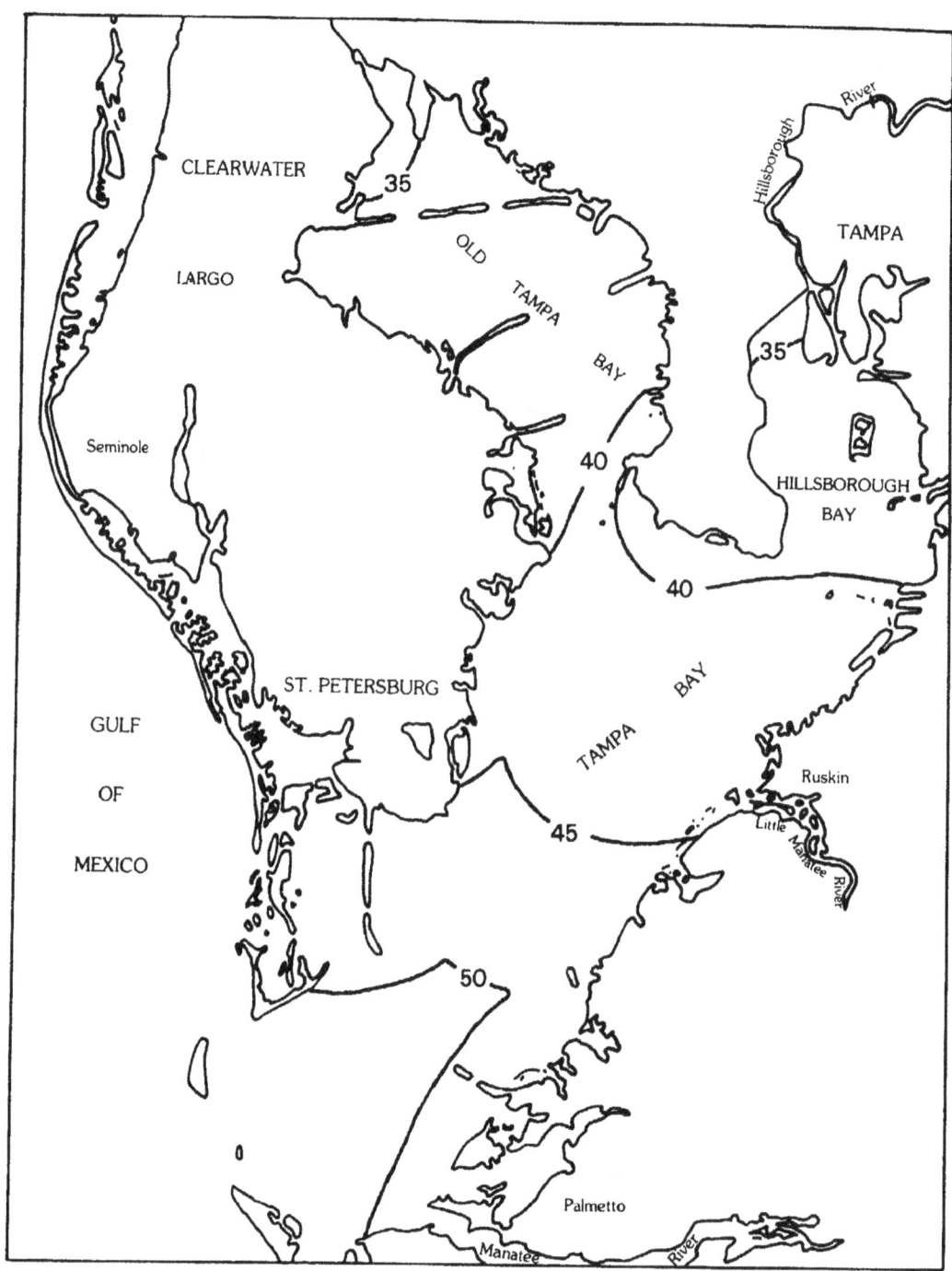

Figure 5.   Isopleth map of annual specific conductivity (mmhos/cm) for Tampa Bay; 5-year mean, Sept. 1978 - Aug. 1983 (data from Hillsborough County Environmental Protection Commission 1983).

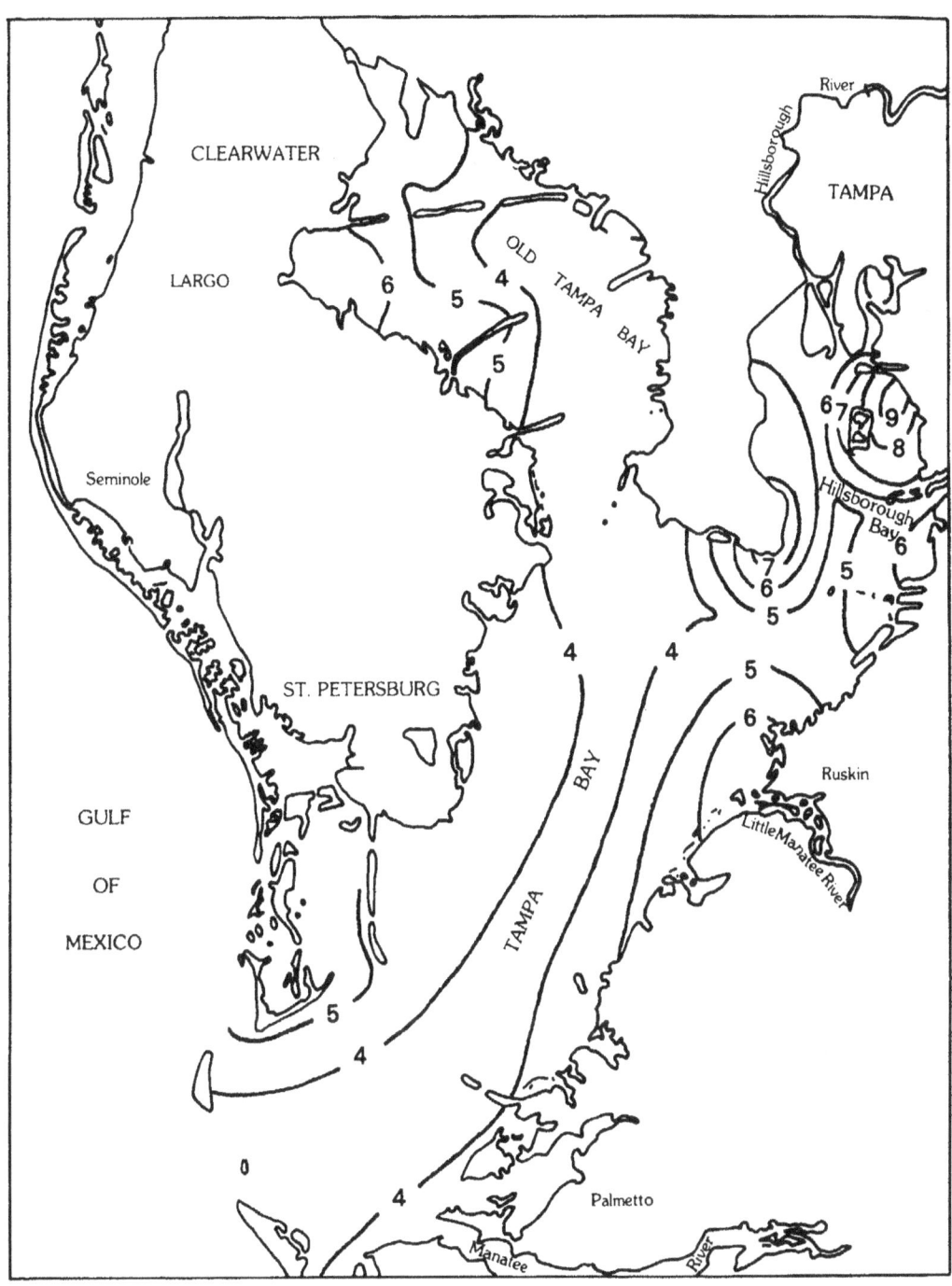

Figure 6. Isopleth map of annual turbidity (NTU's) for Tampa Bay;
5-year mean, Sept. 1978 - Aug. 1983 (data from Hillsborough County
Environmental Protection Commission 1983).

Fahrenheit (°F) or in degrees Celsius (°C). A 16-year mean monthly plot of water temperature for the NOS tide station at the St. Petersburg Municipal Pier is shown in Figure 7. The maximum observed surface water temperature was 90.1 °F (32.2 °C), and the minimum observed water temperature was 52.3 °F (11.3 °C). Fish kills often result from rapid temperature decreases associated with sudden prolonged occurrences of Arctic air masses during the late fall or early winter. During these periods, the water temperature will often drop below the above-listed minimum in shallow water areas. A massive fish kill in January of 1977 was associated with record low bay water temperatures. An isopleth map of mean annual middepth water temperature for Tampa Bay is shown in Figure 8.

3.5.6 Total Nitrogen

Total nitrogen is the sum of all the nitrogen compounds found in a water sample and is measured in milligrams per liter (mg/l). The highest concentrations of total nitrogen are found in Hillsborough Bay. The principal sources of total nitrogen are urban runoff, agricultural runoff, industrial and domestic waste, and rainfall.

Maximum nitrogen levels occur in the late summer and early fall and minimum levels in the late fall. An isopleth map of mean annual total nitrogen levels in Tampa Bay is shown in Figure 9.

3.5.7 Hillsborough County Environmental Protection Commission Water Quality Stations

Hillsborough County operates 81 water quality sampling stations with a period of record of greater than 5 years. Sixty-five of these stations are in the study area and are mapped on the atlas maps.

3.6 BATHYMETRY

Tampa Bay is a drowned river valley. An old submerged Pleistocene river delta is located west of Mullet Key. The Hillsborough River became an entrenched stream during this earlier sea-level stand, and portions of this entrenchment are still reflected in the bathymetry south of the interbay Peninsula and north of Egmont (see Figure 10).

Most of the bottom features in Tampa Bay represent surficial sand wave deposits. Major concentrations of hard rock outcroppings are south of the interbay Peninsula where submarine limestone cliffs line an old Pleistocene entrenched stream bed under Gandy Bridge and offshore from Bishop's Harbor and Rattlesnake Key.

Three main submarine physiographic regions are located in the Tampa Bay complex. They are shallow marine grass and sand flats with average depths of approximately 4 ft, slopes adjacent to the flats ranging in depth from 4 to 20 ft, and deep tidal channels greater than 20 ft deep. Twenty percent of the bay complex is less than 6 ft in water depth. Fifty percent of the bay bottom lies between 6 and 18 ft, and 30% is greater then 18 ft deep (Goodell and Gorsline 1961). The average depth of the Tampa Bay complex is 11.4 ft (McNulty et al.

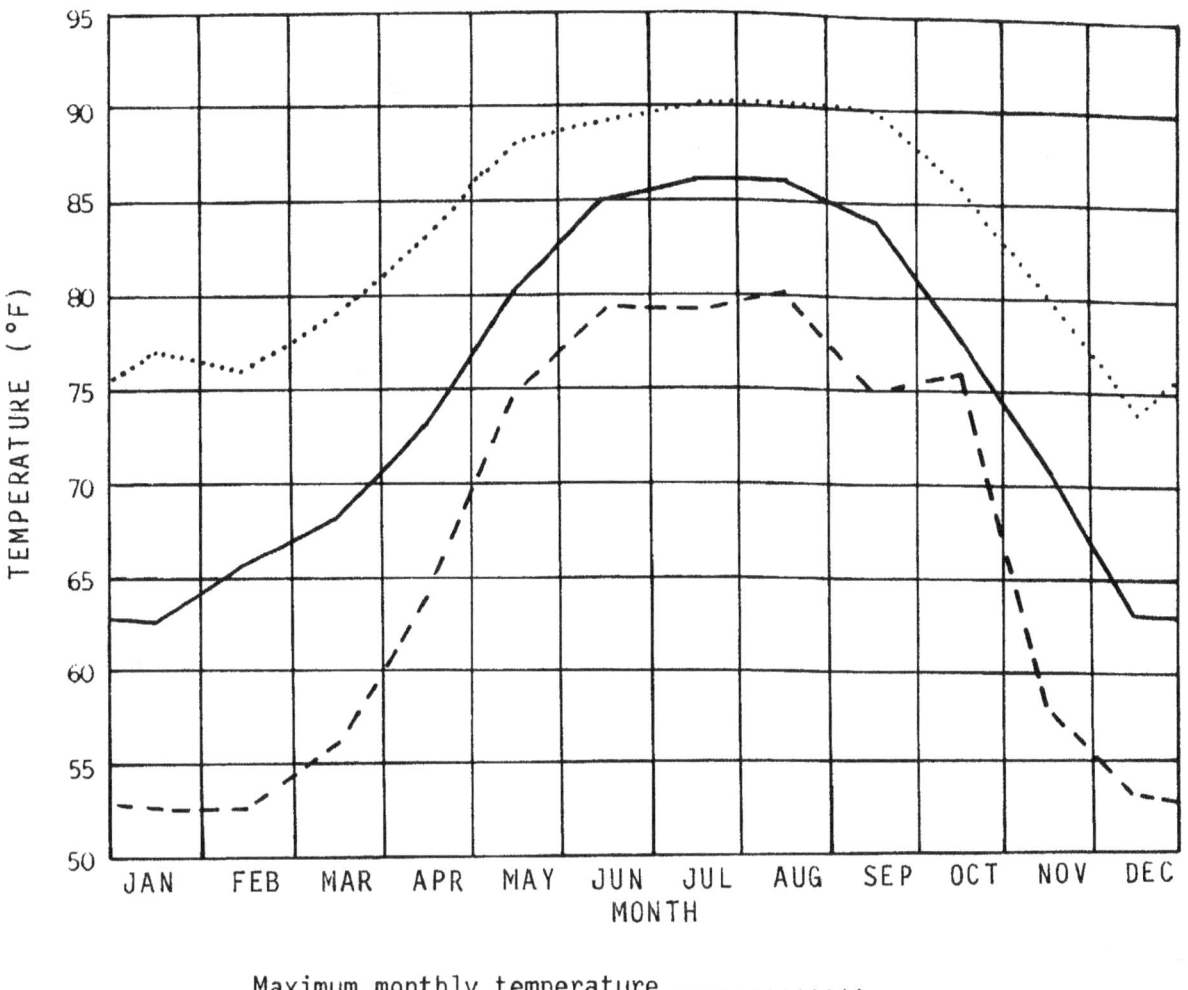

Maximum monthly temperature ....

Mean monthly temperature _____

Minimum monthly temperature — — — — —

Figure 7. Monthly water temperatures for St. Petersburg, Florida, 1947 - 1962 (McNulty et al. 1972).

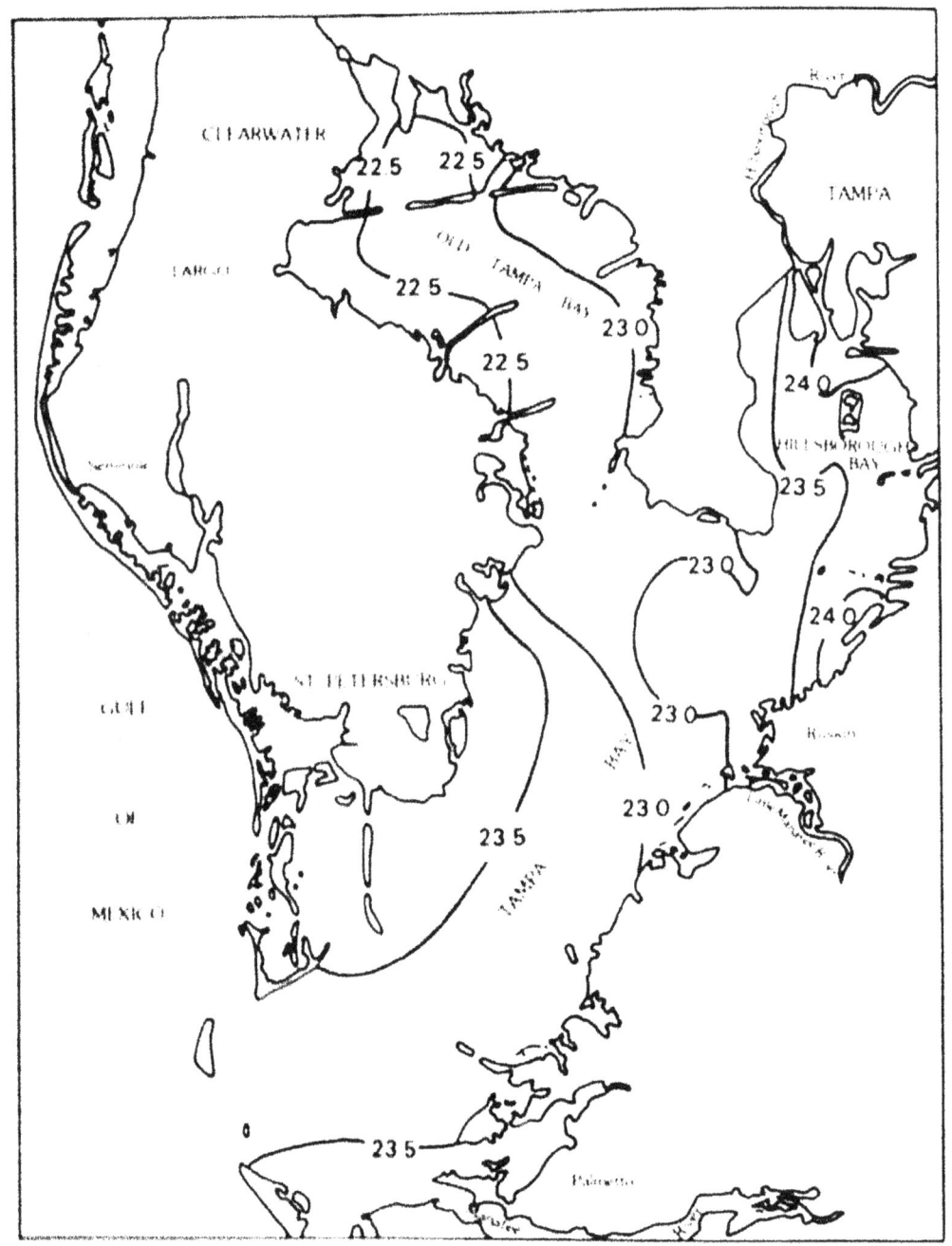

Figure 8. Isopleth map of annual middepth water temperature (°C) for Tampa Bay; 5-year mean, Sept. 1978 - Aug. 1983 (data from Hillsborough County Environmental Protection Commission 1983).

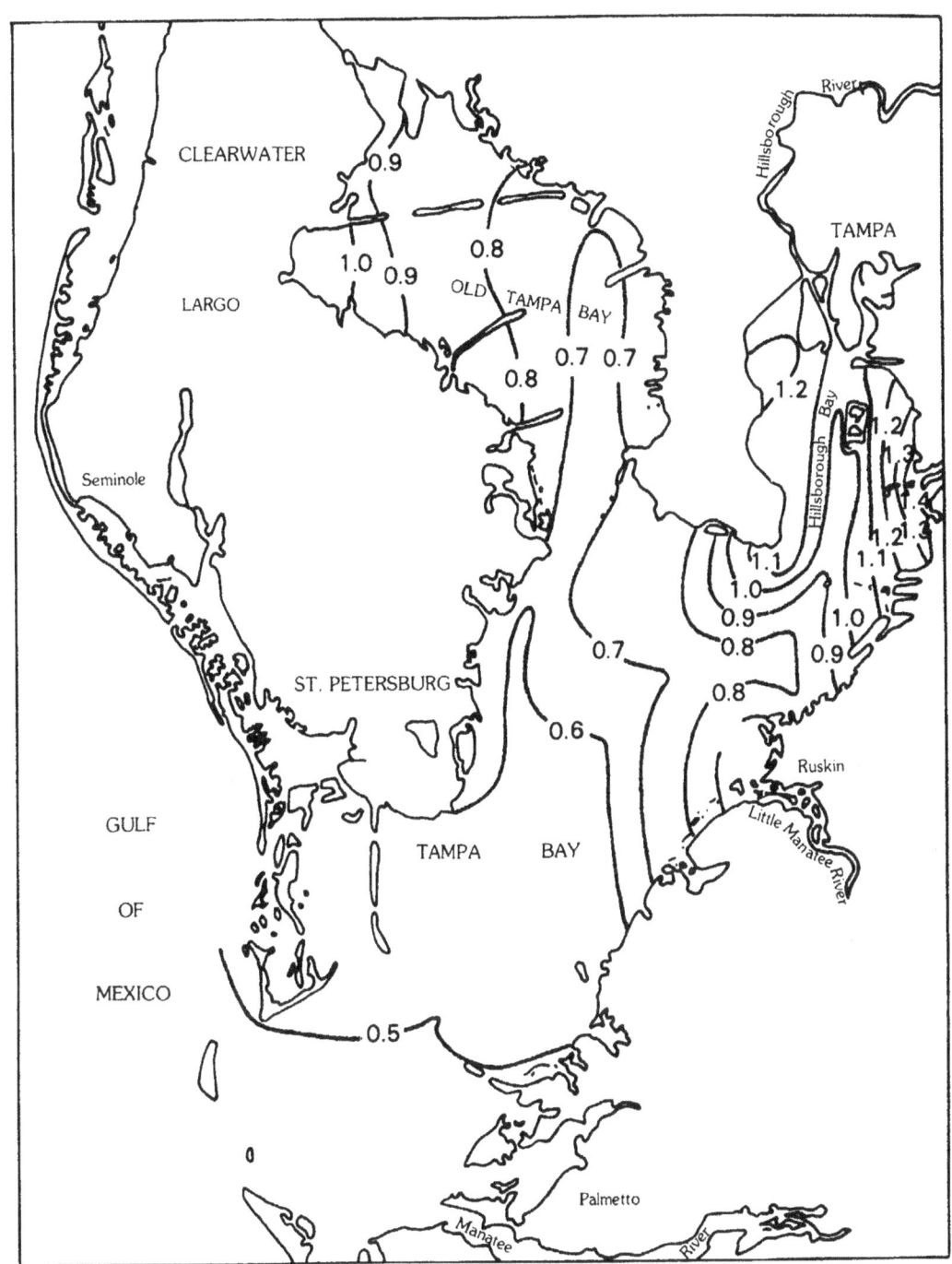

Figure 9. Isopleth map of annual total nitrogen (mg/l) for Tampa Bay; 5-year mean, Sept. 1978 - Aug. 1983 (data from Hillsborough County Environmental Protection Commission 1983).

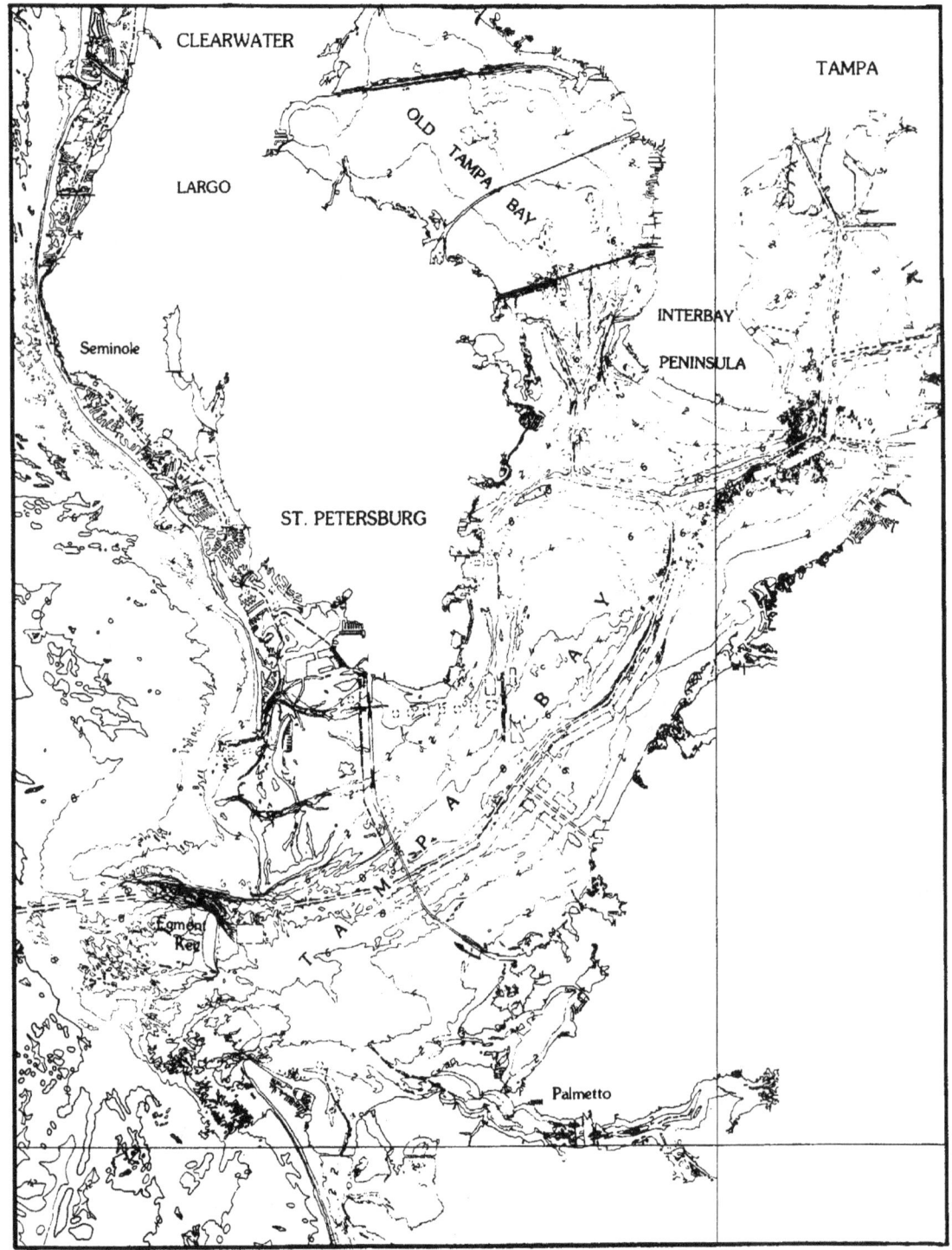

Figure 10. Example of a bathymetric map of Tampa Bay (1:250,000 scale); 2-m contour interval (NOS 1976).

1972). The total surface area at mean high water is 346.0 mi^2 (Lewis and Whitman 1954).

A 2.0-m bathymetric contour interval is used on the individual atlas maps with an initial 1.0-m supplemental contour line used to denote shoals. The bathymetry was compiled by the author and represents an update on the 1976 NOS map for the region.

Boca Ciega Bay lies just north of the Tampa Bay complex and represents a small, shallow lagoon behind the coastal barrier islands. Its average water depth is only 6.6 ft (mhw) (McNulty et al. 1972). Immediately to the north of Boca Ciega Bay lies St. Joseph's Sound, which is another small, shallow lagoon behind the coastal barrier islands. Its average water depth is 4.9 ft (mhw) (McNulty et al. 1972). Sarasota Bay lies just south of the mouth of Tampa Bay. It is a small, shallow lagoon lying behind the coastal barrier islands with an average water depth of 5.5 ft (mhw) (McNulty et al. 1972).

3.7 INTERTIDAL ZONE

The intertidal zone is a region of saltwater marshes and tidal flats that surround Tampa Bay. It is demarcated on the individual atlas overlay maps and was determined from the latest NOS nautical charts for the region.

The intertidal zone is a important buffer zone for marine organisms and biota in Tampa Bay.

3.8 SEDIMENTS

During the early Holocene, Tampa Bay was a drowned river valley with very little sediment accumulation and an average depth of 30 ft. Sediment accumulation since that time has reduced the average depth of Tampa Bay of 11.4 ft (McNulty et al. 1971).

The Tampa Bay complex is composed of a number of interconnected bays. The three principal bays which make up the "Y"-shaped bay complex are Old Tampa Bay to the northwest, Hillsborough Bay to the northeast, and Tampa Bay to the south.

The sediments in the Tampa Bay complex are uniform in character. They are generally composed of reworked terrace quartz and nearshore sand and biogenic carbonate detritus. The mean size of the sediments increases from the upper to the lower reaches of the bay complex. Organic sediments and clays are prominent, primarily in the upper portions of Hillsborough Bay and in other isolated portions of the bay complex (Goodell and Gorsline 1961).

The coastal littoral drift of sand is to the south in Boca Ciega Bay and to the north, south of the mouth of Tampa Bay. North of Tampa Bay, offshore shoaling is occurring to the southwest of the major passes. South of Tampa Bay, shoaling and accretion are taking place to the northwest of the major passes (Goodell and Gorsline 1961).

41

In the sand and grass flats which make up about 15% of the Tampa Bay complex, the sediments are almost entirely quartz sand. The sediments along the slope environments, which make up more than 60% of Tampa Bay, are composed primarily of coarse sand and mollusk shell fragments. The channel sediments are composed almost entirely of very coarse sand and mullusk shell detritus (Goodell and Gorsline 1961).

A small-scale version of the generalized sediment zones included on the individual atlas maps is shown in Figure 11. The generalized sediment zones portrayed on the individual atlas maps were adapted from Taylor and Saloman (1969). The six major sediment types listed are portrayed by a series of graphic screens.

3.9 TIDAL CURRENTS

Tidal exchange is the major flushing agent in the Tampa Bay complex. River discharge, rainwater runoff, and sewage effluent discharge also contribute to localized flushing.

Daily tides in Tampa Bay are primarily semidiurnal (two high tides and two low tides). Tides follow the moon more closely than the sun, and each lunar or tidal day is about 50 min longer than the solar day. On certain days of the month, the tide becomes diurnal, and only one high and low tide occur during the period of a lunar day. Changes in wind and barometric pressure fluctuations cause variations in sea level from day to day. Strong south-westerly winds associated with low barometric pressure cause tide levels to increase above normal. Strong northeasterly winds, associated with high pressure, cause tide levels to decrease below normal.

Monthly mean sea level exhibits an annual cyclic pattern (see Figure 12). During February, sea level reaches its average annual minimum of 4.02 ft. During September, sea level reaches its average annual maximum of 4.67 ft. The numerical values of each tide height are referenced to the level of the primary bench mark for the St. Petersburg Municipal Pier NOS tide station (Hicks et al. 1983).

Sea level has been increasing slowly in Tampa Bay. The average increase in sea level in Tampa Bay is approximately 0.2 ft in a 34-year period or about 0.005 ft/yr (Hicks et al. 1983). A 34-year plot of the annual yearly means of sea level for the St. Petersburg Municipal Pier NOS tide station is shown in Figure 13. This trend in increasing sea level has been experienced at most NOS tide stations in the United States. Sea level has been increasing in San Francisco since 1855, when tidal records first began. National Ocean Service has found that sea levels have been increasing 0.009 ft/year in the northeast Atlantic coast, 0.005 ft/year in the gulf coast, 0.003 ft/year in the southwest Pacific coast, and decreasing 0.001 ft/year in the Pacific Northwest coast. The overall U.S. trend is for sea level to increase 0.004 ft/year (Hicks et al. 1983). Because of complex meteorological and oceanic interactions, future sea-level changes are not easily predicted.

Tidal currents result from water moving into Tampa Bay during flood tide and out of the bay during ebb tide. Slack tide occurs during periods of

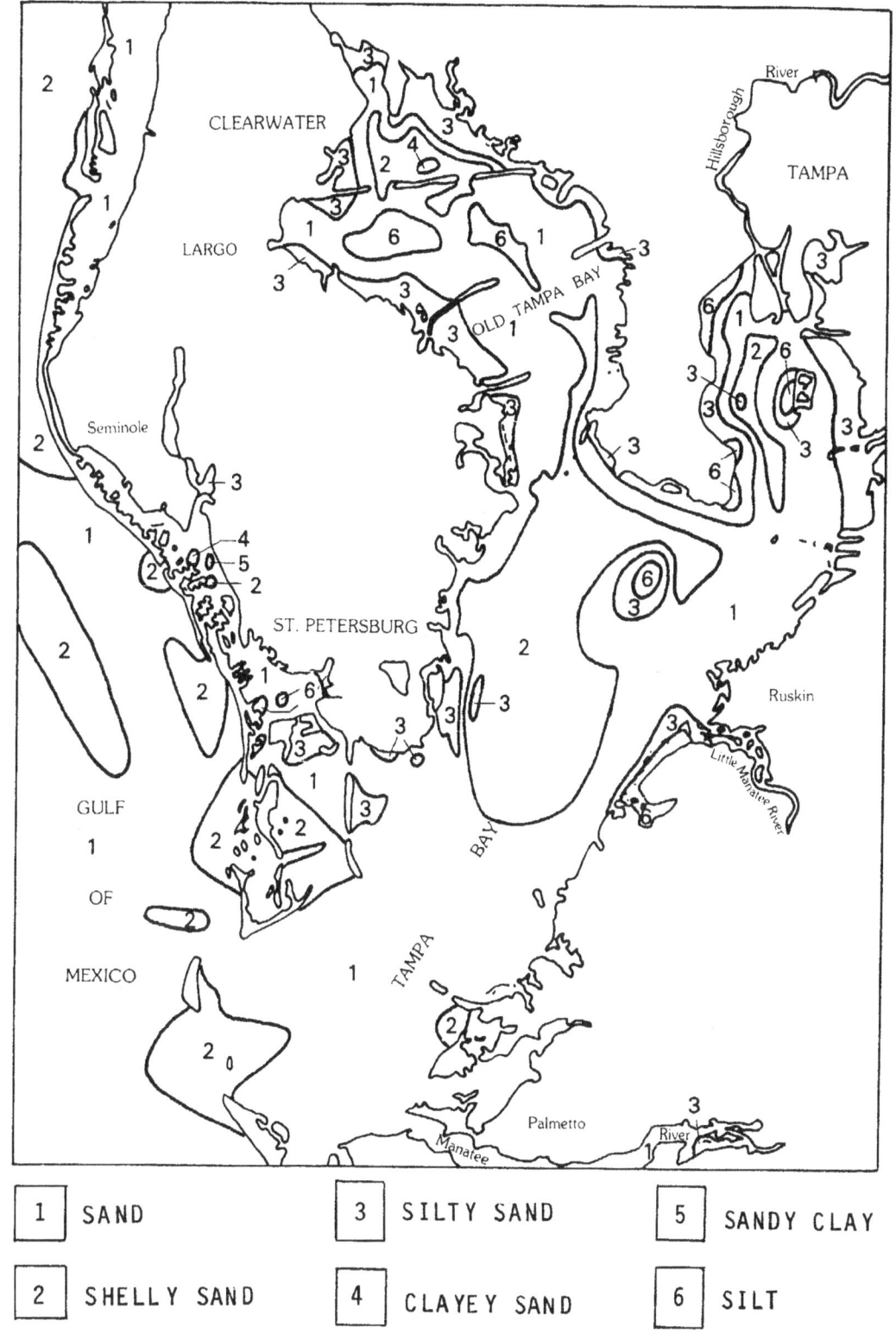

Figure 11. Generalized sediment map of the Tampa Bay area (adapted from Taylor and Saloman 1969).

43

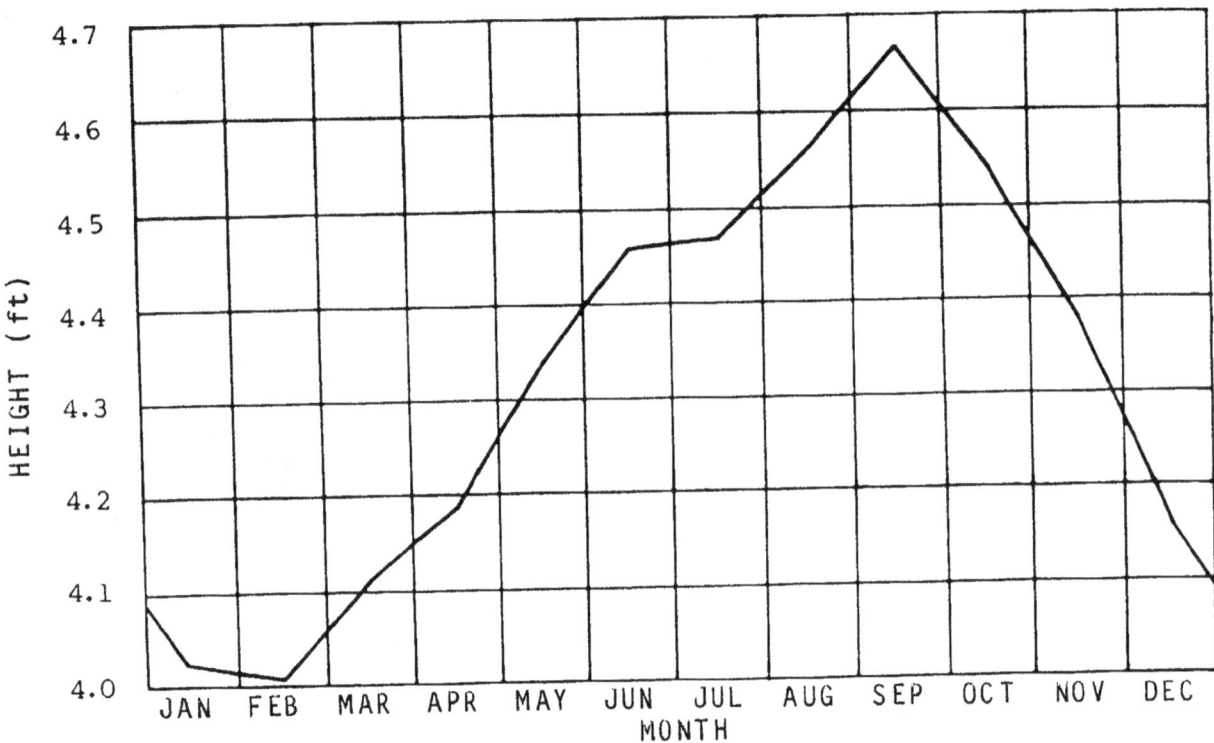

Figure 12. Mean monthly St. Petersburg mean sea level, 1947 - 1980 (Hicks et al. 1983).

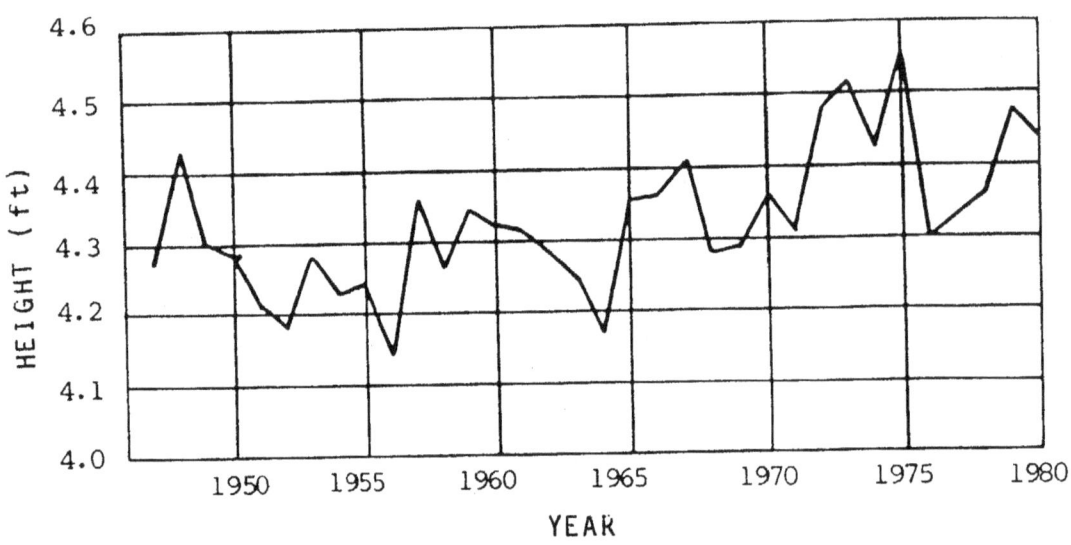

Figure 13. Mean annual St. Petersburg mean sea level, 1947 - 1980 (Hicks et al. 1983).

44

reduced currents between flood and ebb tides. Residual tidal currents are produced by interactions between tidal currents and the bay bottom configuration. Residual currents create long-term water circulation patterns that control or significantly effect the distribution of dissolved and suspended constituents.

Flood, ebb, and circulation patterns computed using a hydrodynamic model developed by the U.S. Geological Survey are shown in Figures 14, 15, and 16 (Goodwin 1984). Figure 15 depicts about 20 large and small circulation features (gyres) within Tampa Bay that are thought to control the rate of constituent flushing.

Residual tidal currents from this model are plotted on the individual 1:24,000-scale atlas maps. A detailed model study of computed particle dispersion done at the University of South Florida indicates that it takes 6 months to affect a 90% reduction in release particles within Tampa Bay. Particles dispersed in northern Old Tampa Bay may take as long as 20 months to be flushed from the bay (Wilkins 1983).

The resultant flows from the U.S. Geological Survey hydrodynamic model are plotted on the individual 1:24,000-scale atlas maps.

3.10   FRESHWATER-SALTWATER INTERFACE

Increased ground-water withdrawals from industrial, agricultural, and municipal ground water production fields have lowered the potentiometric surface (the level to which water will rise in a tightly cased well) in the Floridan aquifer. The Floridan aquifer is the principal ground-water source in the Tampa Bay study area.

Since freshwater is less dense than saltwater, freshwater from the Floridan aquifer floats on a saltwater wedge which underlies the Florida peninsula. In coastal portions of the Tampa Bay region, chloride concentrations range from less than 25 mg/l to 19,000 mg/l, forming a diffuse transition zone between saltwater and freshwater. Chloride (salt) ions are deposited from seawater moving inland from the neighboring Gulf of Mexico. Potential for saltwater intrusion is the greatest in the late spring (May). Water table levels and the potentiometric surface reach their annual lowest levels at this time, and the potential for saltwalter intrusion is greatest (Causseaux and Fretwell 1982).

For the purposes of this report, the 250 mg/l chloride concentration isopleth (line of equal chloride concentration) has been used to depict the 1979 position of the freshwater-saltwater interface in the Floridan aquifer on the individual atlas maps. A smaller scale version of this map is included in Figure 17.

45

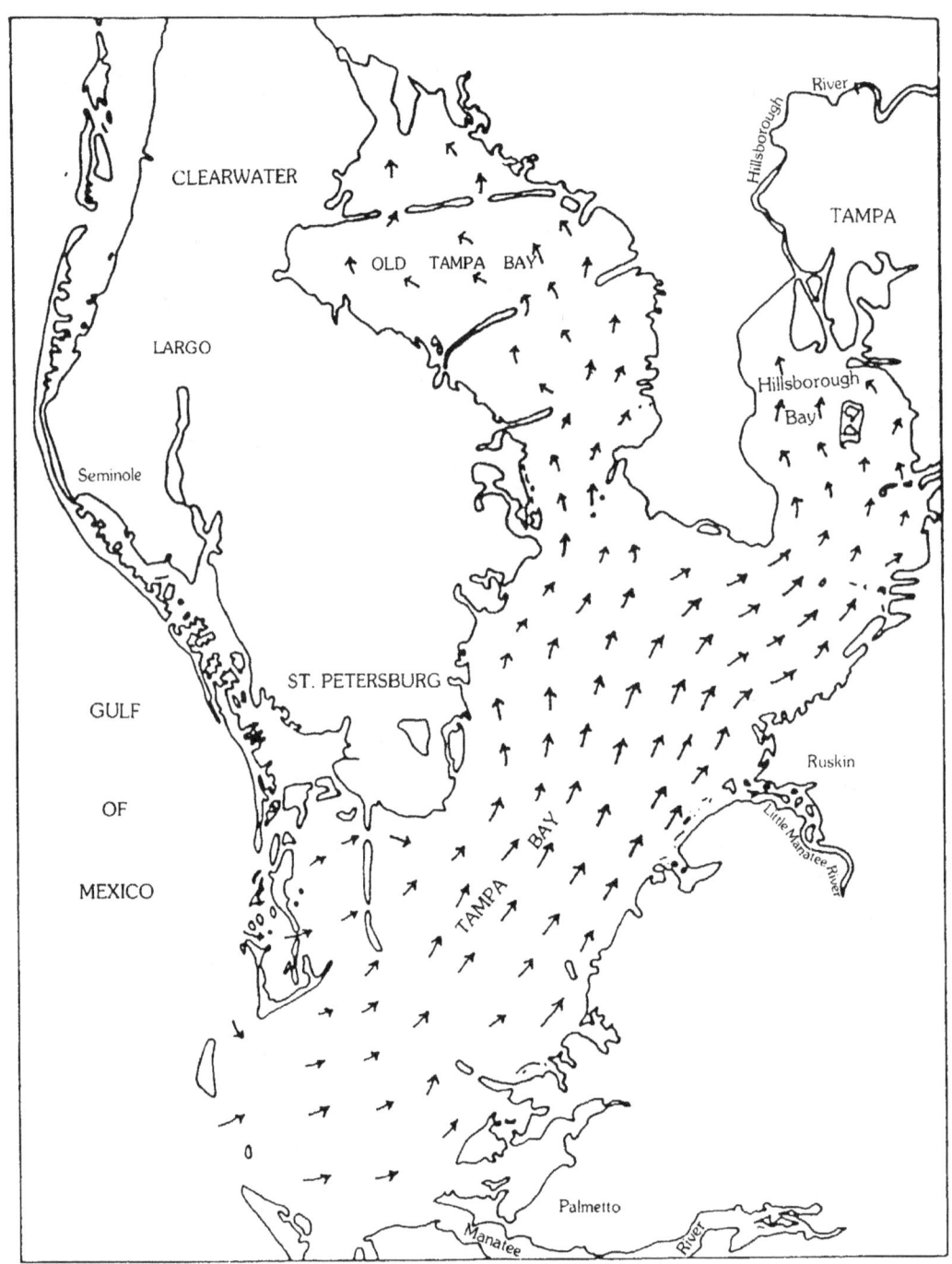

Figure 14. Typical flood tide current flow in Tampa Bay (adapted from Goodwin 1984).

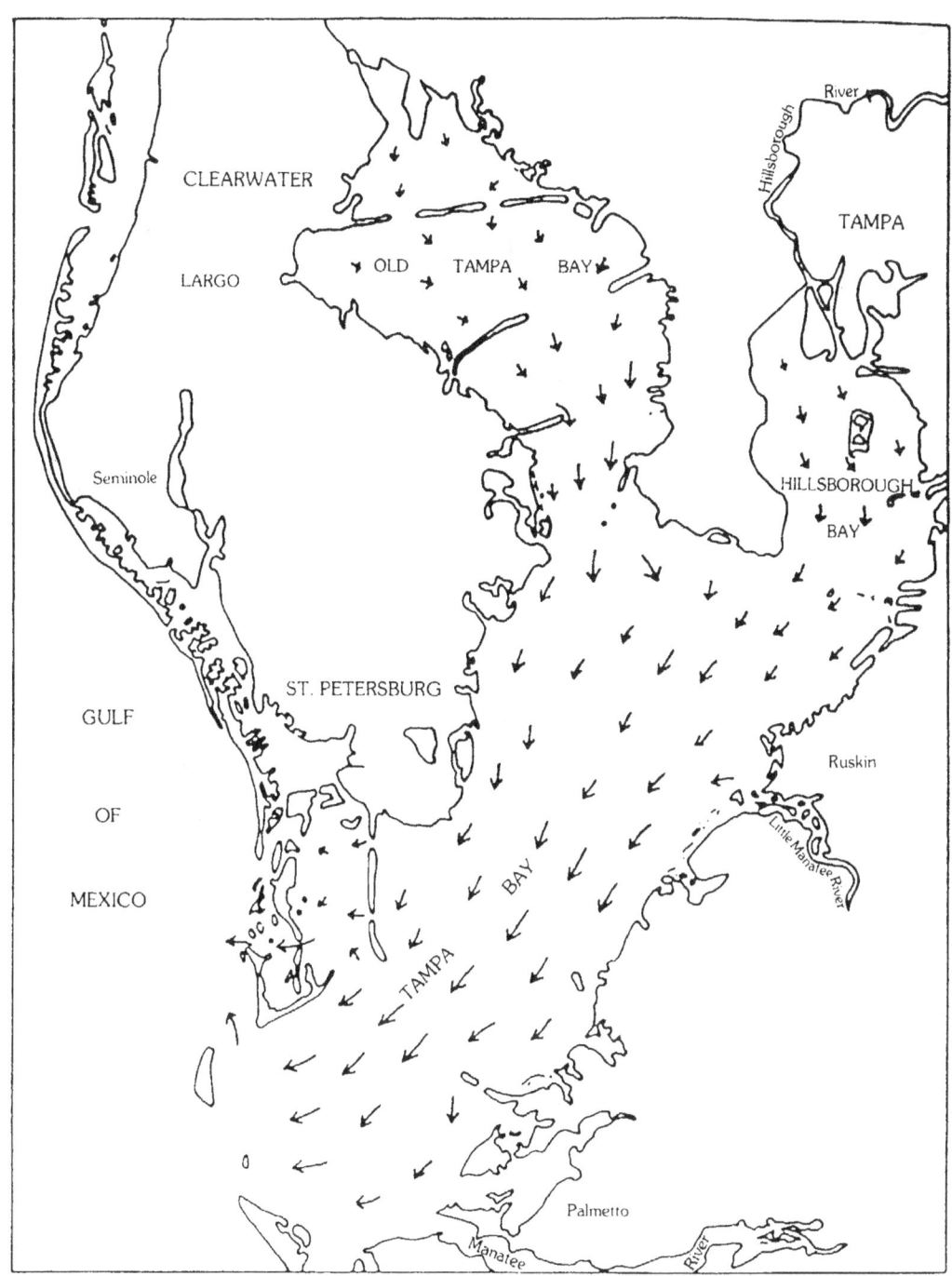

Figure 15. Typical ebb tide current flow in Tampa Bay (adapted from Goodwin 1984).

47

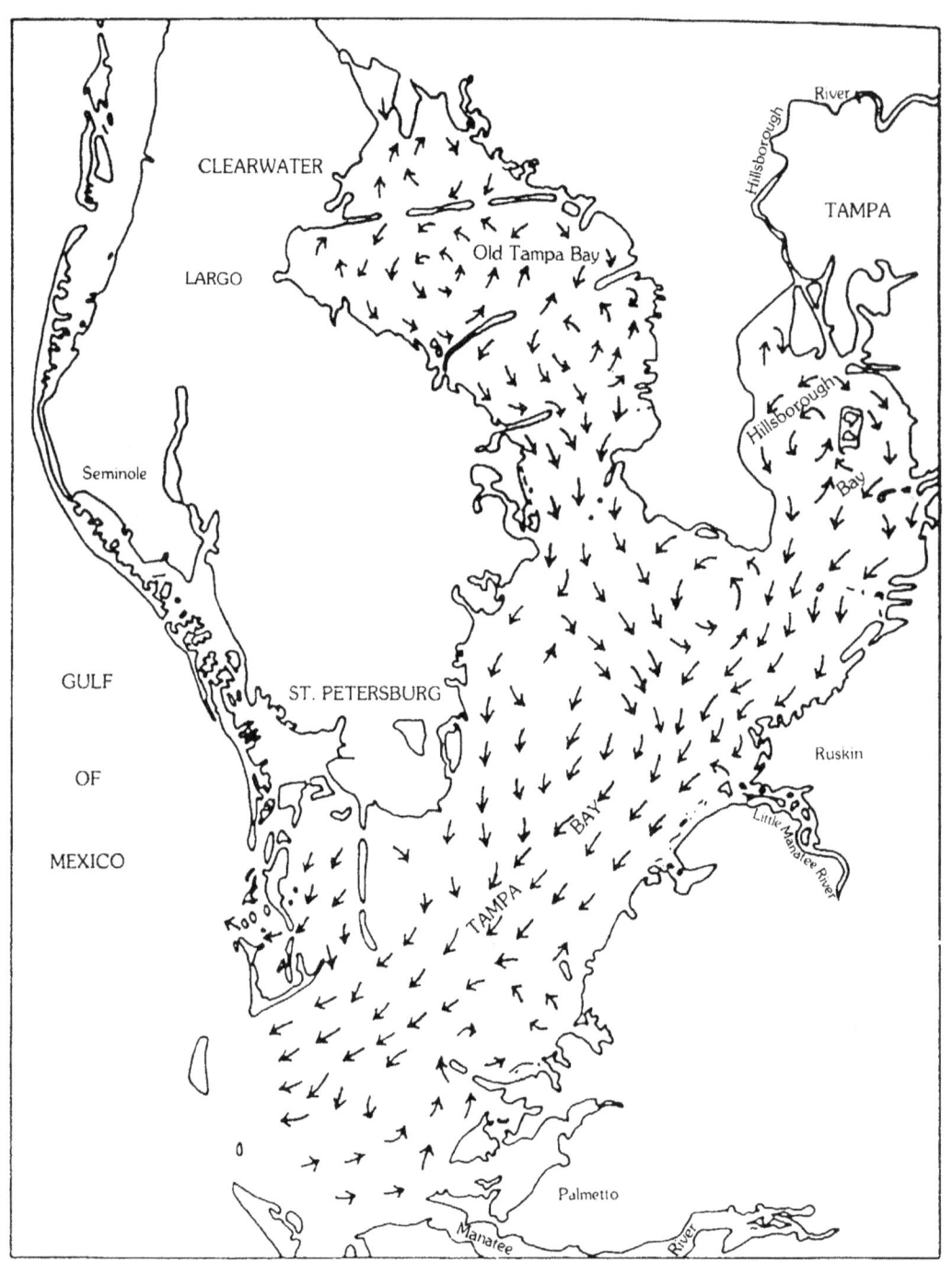

Figure 16. Resultant current flow for one tidal cycle in Tampa Bay
(adapted from Goodwin 1984).

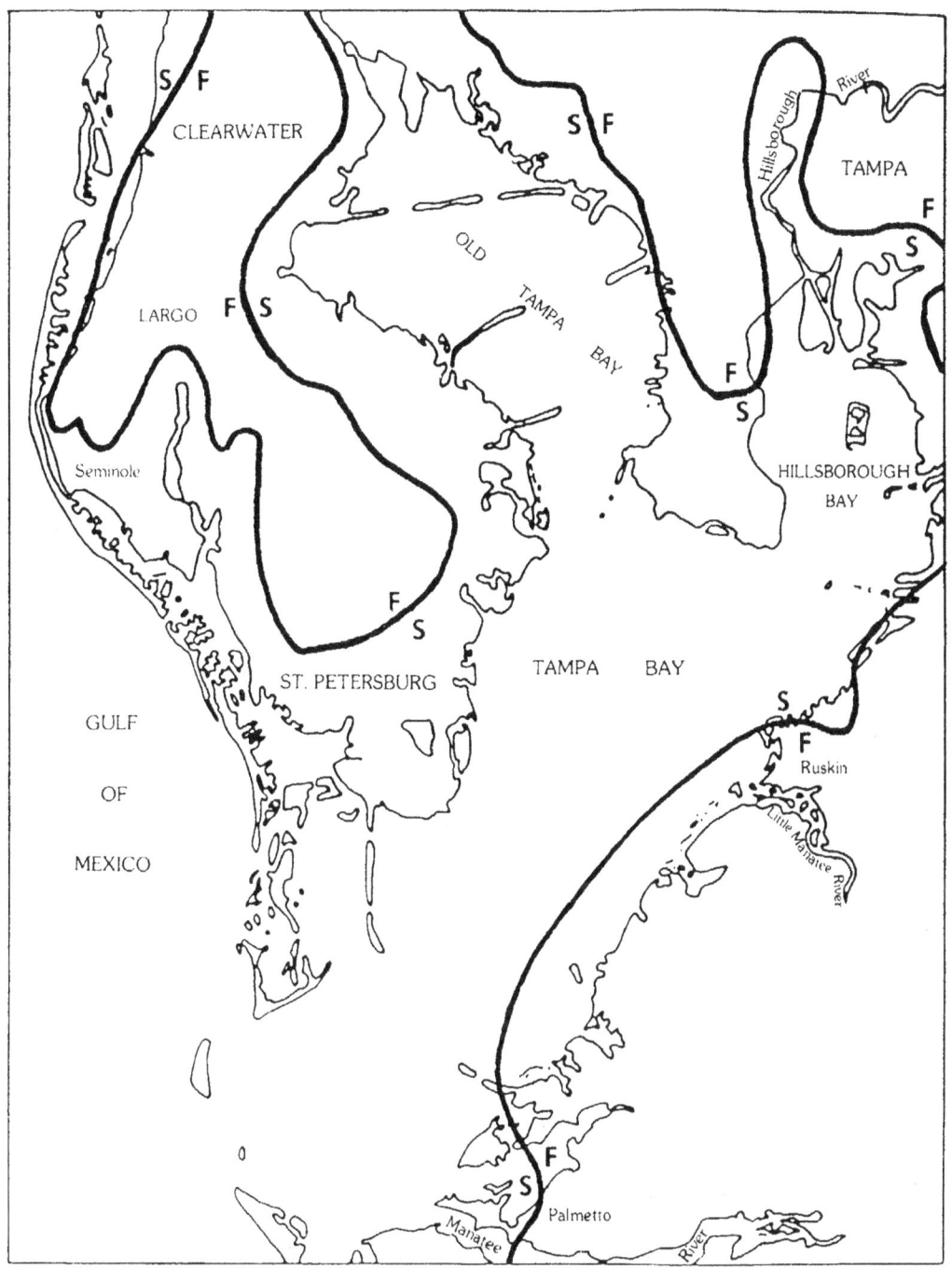

Figure 17. Generalized position of the freshwater-saltwater interface in the upper portion of the Floridan aquifer across the Tampa
Bay area (1979); 250 mg/l-chloride concentration isopleth, or contour
line (Causseaux and Fretwell 1982).

4. APPENDIXES

4.1 APPENDIX A - TAMPA BAY WATER QUALITY STATIONS (5-YR SEASON MEANS), PLOTTED FOR THE ATLAS MAPS.

STATION # 2   LAT. 27°56'25"   LONG. 82°27'42"

PARAMETER	SPRING (3-5)	SUMMER (6-8)	FALL (9-11)	WINTER (12-2)	ANNUAL (1-12)
TOTAL CHLOROPHYLL (µg/l)	31.0	27.5	22.9	25.3	26.7
CONDUCTIVITY (µmhos)	31,267	29,666	28,466	37,300	31,675
TURBIDITY (NTU's)	4.8	4.9	5.8	5.0	5.1
TEMPERATURE (°C)	22.4	29.2	25.6	17.7	23.7
TOTAL NITROGEN (mg/l)	1.15	1.43	1.31	0.94	1.21

STATION # 6   LAT. 27°53'20"   LONG. 82°28'38"

PARAMETER	SPRING (3-5)	SUMMER (6-8)	FALL (9-11)	WINTER (12-2)	ANNUAL (1-12)
TOTAL CHLOROPHYLL (µg/l)	42.3	59.6	37.7	35.6	43.8
CONDUCTIVITY (µmhos)	36,200	35,483	34,033	40,950	36,667
TURBIDITY (NTU's)	8.7	5.7	4.4	5.6	6.1
TEMPERATURE (°C)	21.9	29.1	25.6	17.1	23.4
TOTAL NITROGEN (mg/l)	1.29	1.28	1.33	0.90	1.20

STATION # 7   LAT. 27°51'21"   LONG. 82°27'37"

PARAMETER	SPRING (3-5)	SUMMER (6-8)	FALL (9-11)	WINTER (12-2)	ANNUAL (1-12)
TOTAL CHLOROPHYLL (µg/l)	47.5	53.1	41.7	44.0	46.6
CONDUCTIVITY (µmhos)	36,700	36,967	34,600	41,283	37,388
TURBIDITY (NTU's)	8.8	6.2	5.7	5.6	6.6
TEMPERATURE (°C)	22.4	29.1	25.7	17.0	23.6
TOTAL NITROGEN (mg/l)	1.29	1.21	1.17	0.82	1.12

STATION # 8   LAT. 27°51'00"   LONG. 82°24'57"

PARAMETER	SPRING (3-5)	SUMMER (6-8)	FALL (9-11)	WINTER (12-2)	ANNUAL (1-12)
TOTAL CHLOROPHYLL (µg/l)	46.8	116.7	48.6	38.8	62.7
CONDUCTIVITY (µmhos)	36,500	36,883	32,733	39,250	36,342
TURBIDITY (NTU's)	7.7	7.6	6.7	6.6	7.2
TEMPERATURE (°C)	22.7	29.8	25.6	17.6	23.9
TOTAL NITROGEN (mg/l)	1.33	1.65	1.46	0.90	1.34

STATION # 9   LAT. 27°47'06"   LONG. 82°25'46"

PARAMETER	SPRING (3-5)	SUMMER (6-8)	FALL (9-11)	WINTER (12-2)	ANNUAL (1-12)
TOTAL CHLOROPHYLL (µg/l)	43.0	40.8	32.6	29.7	36.5
CONDUCTIVITY (µmhos)	40,134	40,650	37,933	42,600	40,329
TURBIDITY (NTU's)	7.8	5.3	3.7	3.9	5.2
TEMPERATURE (°C)	23.0	29.8	26.3	18.0	24.3
TOTAL NITROGEN (mg/l)	1.06	1.01	1.23	0.69	1.00

50

STATION # 11   LAT. 27°48'46"   LONG. 82°29'03"

PARAMETER	SPRING (3-5)	SUMMER (6-8)	FALL (9-11)	WINTER (12-2)	ANNUAL (1-12)
TOTAL CHLOROPHYLL (µg/l)	42.8	55.1	36.1	18.1	38.0
CONDUCTIVITY (µmhos)	39,133	39,383	36,633	43,63	39,696
TURBIDITY (NTU's)	7.6	8.0	6.4	7.0	7.2
TEMPERATURE (°C)	21.9	29.0	25.6	16.4	23.2
TOTAL NITROGEN (mg/l)	1.10	1.45	1.32	0.81	1.17

STATION #13   LAT. 27°48'45"   LONG. 82°31'25"

PARAMETER	SPRING (3-5)	SUMMER (6-8)	FALL (9-11)	WINTER (12-2)	ANNUAL (1-12)
TOTAL CHLOROPHYLL (µg/l)	27.6	33.3	34.1	18.1	28.3
CONDUCTIVITY (µmhos)	41,250	40,702	39,100	36,073	39,281
TURBIDITY (NTU's)	3.8	4.1	2.8	2.8	3.4
TEMPERATURE (°C)	21.9	29.2	24.9	15.6	22.9
TOTAL NITROGEN (mg/l)	0.77	0.81	0.82	0.58	0.75

STATION #14   LAT. 27°46'55"   LONG. 82°31'25"

PARAMETER	SPRING (3-5)	SUMMER (6-8)	FALL (9-11)	WINTER (12-2)	ANNUAL (1-12)
TOTAL CHLOROPHYLL (µg/l)	31.5	32.3	24.9	20.2	27.2
CONDUCTIVITY (µmhos)	43,767	42,317	39,600	43,533	42,304
TURBIDITY (NTU's)	4.6	5.6	2.6	3.3	4.0
TEMPERATURE (°C)	22.1	29.2	25.7	16.6	23.4
TOTAL NITROGEN (mg/l)	0.93	0.75	0.95	0.56	0.80

STATION #16   LAT. 27°43'21"   LONG. 82°32'05"

PARAMETER	SPRING (3-5)	SUMMER (6-8)	FALL (9-11)	WINTER (12-2)	ANNUAL (1-12)
TOTAL CHLOROPHYLL (µg/l)	23.9	20.2	20.8	16.1	20.2
CONDUCTIVITY (µmhos)	42,650	44,238	42,833	45,308	43,757
TURBIDITY (NTU's)	5.1	3.5	3.6	4.1	4.1
TEMPERATURE (°C)	22.2	29.5	24.8	16.1	23.2
TOTAL NITROGEN (mg/l)	0.69	0.65	0.81	0.53	0.67

STATION #19   LAT. 27°41'59"   LONG. 82°32'59"

PARAMETER	SPRING (3-5)	SUMMER (6-8)	FALL (9-11)	WINTER (12-2)	ANNUAL (1-12)
TOTAL CHLOROPHYLL (µg/l)	23.5	17.1	20.3	14.0	18.7
CONDUCTIVITY (µmhos)	44,267	45,482	43,666	46,913	45,082
TURBIDITY (NTU's)	4.5	3.1	2.9	2.9	3.4
TEMPERATURE (°C)	22.2	29.5	24.6	16.3	23.2
TOTAL NITROGEN (mg/l)	0.50	0.62	0.76	0.41	0.57

STATION #21   LAT. 27°40'06"   LONG. 82°33'04"

PARAMETER	SPRING (3-5)	SUMMER (6-8)	FALL (9-11)	WINTER (12-2)	ANNUAL (1-12)
TOTAL CHLOROPHYLL (µg/l)	21.4	19.4	21.8	12.6	18.8
CONDUCTIVITY (µmhos)	45,400	46,954	45,566	48,157	46,519
TURBIDITY (NTU's)	4.7	6.8	3.9	3.3	4.7
TEMPERATURE (°C)	22.2	29.6	25.1	16.3	24.7
TOTAL NITROGEN (mg/l)	0.41	0.54	0.87	0.38	0.55

STATION #23   LAT. 27°39'50"   LONG. 82°35'52"

PARAMETER	SPRING (3-5)	SUMMER (6-8)	FALL (9-11)	WINTER (12-2)	ANNUAL (1-12)
TOTAL CHLOROPHYLL (µg/l)	20.8	16.1	20.6	11.7	17.3
CONDUCTIVITY (µmhos)	47,100	47,460	46,366	50,283	47,802
TURBIDITY (NTU's)	4.0	2.2	3.7	3.4	3.3
TEMPERATURE (°C)	27.2	29.7	25.4	16.5	24.7
TOTAL NITROGEN (mg/l)	0.60	0.53	0.60	0.42	0.54

STATION #24   LAT. 27°35'01"   LONG. 82°37'01"

PARAMETER	SPRING (3-5)	SUMMER (6-8)	FALL (9-11)	WINTER (12-2)	ANNUAL (1-13)
TOTAL CHLOROPHYLL (µg/l)	19.8	16.2	19.3	11.9	16.8
CONDUCTIVITY (µmhos)	46,633	48,137	47,066	49,945	47,945
TURBIDITY (NTU's)	4.0	3.2	3.5	3.7	3.6
TEMPERATURE (°C)	22.7	29.4	24.9	16.5	23.4
TOTAL NITROGEN (mg/l)	0.46	0.56	0.79	0.35	0.54

STATION #25   LAT. 27°39'13"   LONG. 82°40'13"

PARAMETER	SPRING (3-5)	SUMMER (6-8)	FALL (9-11)	WINTER (12-2)	ANNUAL (1-13)
TOTAL CHLOROPHYLL (µg/l)	19.0	20.8	26.7	11.2	19.4
CONDUCTIVITY (µmhos)	46,983	47,555	47,266	51,095	48,225
TURBIDITY (NTU's)	4.8	4.0	5.4	3.6	4.4
TEMPERATURE (°C)	22.9	30.0	25.0	16.6	23.6
TOTAL NITROGEN (mg/l)	0.51	0.53	0.65	0.39	0.52

STATION #28   LAT. 27°42'28"   LONG. 82°36'34"

PARAMETER	SPRING (3-5)	SUMMER (6-8)	FALL (9-11)	WINTER (12-2)	ANNUAL (1-13)
TOTAL CHLOROPHYLL (µg/l)	24.6	28.5	26.8	14.6	23.6
CONDUCTIVITY (µmhos)	47,333	44,044	41,633	47,958	45,242
TURBIDITY (NTU's)	5.1	4.6	3.8	3.2	4.2
TEMPERATURE (°C)	22.8	29.5	25.4	16.7	23.6
TOTAL NITROGEN (mg/l)	0.53	0.65	0.76	0.51	0.61

STATION #32   LAT. 27°47'34"   LONG. 82°34'15"

PARAMETER	SPRING (3-5)	SUMMER (6-8)	FALL (9-11)	WINTER (12-2)	ANNUAL (1-13)
TOTAL CHLOROPHYLL (µg/l)	29.2	32.5	27.5	18.0	26.8
CONDUCTIVITY (µmhos)	41,950	39,533	39,400	44,000	41,221
TURBIDITY (NTU's)	4.7	4.0	2.8	2.7	3.6
TEMPERATURE (°C)	21.8	29.0	24.8	15.5	22.8
TOTAL NITROGEN (mg/l)	0.67	0.79	0.89	0.54	0.72

STATION #33   LAT. 27°49'14"   LONG. 82°34'15"

PARAMETER	SPRING (3-5)	SUMMER (6-8)	FALL (9-11)	WINTER (12-2)	ANNUAL (1-13)
TOTAL CHLOROPHYLL (µg/l)	27.9	32.8	28.9	18.3	27.0
CONDUCTIVITY (µmhos)	41,600	39,883	33,317	42,400	40,550
TURBIDITY (NTU's)	4.5	3.2	2.8	2.9	3.4
TEMPERATURE (°C)	21.8	29.1	24.9	15.3	22.8
TOTAL NITROGEN (mg/l)	0.62	0.73	0.88	0.55	0.69

STATION #36   LAT. 27°51'35"   LONG. 82°33'13"

PARAMETER	SPRING (3-5)	SUMMER (6-8)	FALL (9-11)	WINTER (12-2)	ANNUAL (1-13)
TOTAL CHLOROPHYLL (µg/l)	27.5	42.0	30.4	27.0	31.7
CONDUCTIVITY (µmhos)	40,833	39,664	37,900	43,200	40,399
TURBIDITY (NTU's)	4.0	4.2	2.9	2.4	3.4
TEMPERATURE (°C)	21.7	29.1	24.8	15.5	22.8
TOTAL NITROGEN (mg/l)	0.63	0.71	0.84	0.46	0.66

STATION #38   LAT. 27°52'54"   LONG. 82°34'40"

PARAMETER	SPRING (3-5)	SUMMER (6-8)	FALL (9-11)	WINTER (12-2)	ANNUAL (1-12)
TOTAL CHLOROPHYLL (µg/l)	24.1	31.0	30.7	16.4	25.6
CONDUCTIVITY (µmhos)	39,700	37,836	36,583	40,542	38,665
TURBIDITY (NTU's)	3.9	3.9	3.2	2.4	3.4
TEMPERATURE (°C)	21.9	29.3	24.8	15.2	22.8
TOTAL NITROGEN (mg/l)	0.62	0.80	0.88	0.45	0.69

STATION #40   LAT. 27°55'45"   LONG. 82°35'00"

PARAMETER	SPRING (3-5)	SUMMER (6-8)	FALL (9-11)	WINTER (12-2)	ANNUAL (1-12)
TOTAL CHLOROPHYLL (µg/l)	25.0	28.0	35.1	18.2	26.6
CONDUCTIVITY (µmhos)	39,167	37,057	35,283	40,533	38,010
TURBIDITY (NTU's)	4.5	5.0	3.2	2.1	3.7
TEMPERATURE (°C)	21.6	29.0	24.7	15.4	22.7
TOTAL NITROGEN (mg/l)	0.68	0.86	0.85	0.58	0.74

STATION #41   LAT. 27°56'15"   LONG. 82°33'54"

PARAMETER	SPRING (3-5)	SUMMER (6-8)	FALL (9-11)	WINTER (12-2)	ANNUAL (1-12)
TOTAL CHLOROPHYLL (µg/l)	21.6	28.8	31.0	15.2	24.2
CONDUCTIVITY (µmhos)	39,117	37,165	36,067	41,033	38,346
TURBIDITY (NTU's)	4.2	3.7	3.2	1.9	3.2
TEMPERATURE (°C)	22.0	29.7	25.0	15.6	23.1
TOTAL NITROGEN (mg/l)	0.59	0.73	0.81	0.49	0.66

STATION #44   LAT. 27°55'38"   LONG. 82°28'37"

PARAMETER	SPRING (3-5)	SUMMER (6-8)	FALL (9-11)	WINTER (12-2)	ANNUAL (1-12)
TOTAL CHLOROPHYLL (µg/l)	37.8	57.1	45.7	32.6	43.3
CONDUCTIVITY (µmhos)	34,567	32,400	32,500	39,167	34,658
TURBIDITY (NTU's)	6.0	4.8	4.2	5.7	5.2
TEMPERATURE (°C)	21.9	28.6	25.5	17.0	23.2
TOTAL NITROGEN (mg/l)	1.11	1.32	1.44	0.82	1.17

STATION #46   LAT. 27°59'22"   LONG. 82°39'29"

PARAMETER	SPRING (3-5)	SUMMER (6-8)	FALL (9-11)	WINTER (12-2)	ANNUAL (1-12)
TOTAL CHLOROPHYLL (µg/l)	22.0	31.2	31.6	17.3	25.5
CONDUCTIVITY (µmhos)	36,617	34,109	32,783	33,400	35,477
TURBIDITY (NTU's)	6.4	8.5	5.2	3.0	5.8
TEMPERATURE (°C)	22.0	29.0	24.9	14.7	22.6
TOTAL NITROGEN (mg/l)	0.70	1.03	1.04	0.71	0.87

STATION #47   LAT. 27°58'20"   LONG. 82°37'13"

PARAMETER	SPRING (3-5)	SUMMER (6-8)	FALL (9-11)	WINTER (12-2)	ANNUAL (1-12)
TOTAL CHLOROPHYLL (µg/l)	22.3	28.4	31.4	16.5	24.6
CONDUCTIVITY (µmhos)	37,267	35,371	33,933	39,300	36,468
TURBIDITY (NTU's)	5.6	5.6	3.8	2.6	4.4
TEMPERATURE (°C)	21.6	28.9	24.2	14.8	22.4
TOTAL NITROGEN (mg/l)	0.85	0.85	0.87	0.67	0.81

STATION #50   LAT. 27°55'07"   LONG. 82°32'16"

PARAMETER	SPRING (3-5)	SUMMER (6-8)	FALL (9-11)	WINTER (12-2)	ANNUAL (1-12)
TOTAL CHLOROPHYLL (µg/l)	20.3	29.0	29.2	15.8	23.6
CONDUCTIVITY (µmhos)	39,933	38,489	36,800	42,033	39,314
TURBIDITY (NTU's)	3.3	3.9	2.8	2.0	3.0
TEMPERATURE (°C)	22.2	29.7	25.1	15.6	23.2
TOTAL NITROGEN (mg/l)	0.69	0.83	0.71	0.54	0.69

STATION #51   LAT. 27°53'30"   LONG. 82°32'35"

PARAMETER	SPRING (3-5)	SUMMER (6-8)	FALL (9-11)	WINTER (12-2)	ANNUAL (1-12)
TOTAL CHLOROPHYLL (µg/l)	27.5	33.6	30.3	18.1	27.4
CONDUCTIVITY (µmhos)	40,617	38,265	37,550	42,83	39,816
TURBIDITY (NTU's)	4.4	3.9	2.7	2.4	3.4
TEMPERATURE (°C)	22.0	29.5	24.9	15.4	23.0
TOTAL NITROGEN (mg/l)	0.72	0.80	0.87	0.63	0.76

STATION #52   LAT. 27°54'15"   LONG. 82°26'07"

PARAMETER	SPRING (3-5)	SUMMER (6-8)	FALL (9-11)	WINTER (12-2)	ANNUAL (1-12)
TOTAL CHLOROPHYLL (µg/l)	46.8	48.3	38.4	35.3	42.2
CONDUCTIVITY (µmhos)	38,125	38,183	37,067	40,817	38,548
TURBIDITY (NTU's)	11.9	4.9	4.7	4.6	6.5
TEMPERATURE (°C)	22.8	30.0	26.5	17.8	24.3
TOTAL NITROGEN (mg/l)	1.15	0.97	1.19	0.86	1.04

STATION #54   LAT. 27°55'59"   LONG. 82°25'57"

PARAMETER	SPRING (3-5)	SUMMER (6-8)	FALL (9-11)	WINTER (12-2)	ANNUAL (1-12)
TOTAL CHLOROPHYLL (µg/l)	31.9	37.0	31.1	25.8	31.4
CONDUCTIVITY (µmhos)	38,133	37,983	36,625	41,383	38,531
TURBIDITY (NTU's)	4.8	3.7	3.6	4.6	4.2
TEMPERATURE (°C)	22.5	30.0	26.0	17.3	24.0
TOTAL NITROGEN (mg/l)	1.01	1.35	1.16	0.82	1.09

STATION #55   LAT. 27°51'09"   LONG. 82°26'07"

PARAMETER	SPRING (3-5)	SUMMER (6-8)	FALL (9-11)	WINTER (12-2)	ANNUAL (1-12)
TOTAL CHLOROPHYLL (µg/l)	36.8	48.4	37.6	37.2	40.0
CONDUCTIVITY (µmhos)	38,033	38,100	36,600	41,150	38,471
TURBIDITY (NTU's)	7.2	5.0	5.2	4.6	5.5
TEMPERATURE (°C)	22.2	29.3	25.6	17.5	23.6
TOTAL NITROGEN (mg/l)	1.19	0.94	1.23	0.78	1.03

STATION #58   LAT. 27°56'20"   LONG. 82°25'07"

PARAMETER	SPRING (3-5)	SUMMER (6-8)	FALL (9-11)	WINTER (12-2)	ANNUAL (1-12)
TOTAL CHLOROPHYLL (µg/l)	46.3	61.5	42.0	49.2	49.8
CONDUCTIVITY (µmhos)	33,593	35,883	32,933	39,033	35,360
TURBIDITY (NTU's)	8.2	5.5	5.4	6.1	6.3
TEMPERATURE (°C)	22.8	29.9	26.0	17.5	24.0
TOTAL NITROGEN (mg/l)	1.18	1.34	1.31	0.98	1.20

STATION #60   LAT. 27°59'18"   LONG. 82°38'01"

PARAMETER	SPRING (3-5)	SUMMER (6-8)	FALL (9-11)	WINTER (12-2)	ANNUAL (1-12)
TOTAL CHLOROPHYLL (µg/l)	21.8	30.7	31.7	16.5	25.2
CONDUCTIVITY (µmhos)	37,042	35,474	33,700	38,767	36,246
TURBIDITY (NTU's)	5.8	6.3	4.4	3.3	5.0
TEMPERATURE (°C)	21.7	29.1	24.2	14.8	22.5
TOTAL NITROGEN (mg/l)	0.71	0.97	1.16	0.59	0.86

STATION #61   LAT. 27°58'06"   LONG. 82°33'37"

PARAMETER	SPRING (3-5)	SUMMER (6-8)	FALL (9-11)	WINTER (12-2)	ANNUAL (1-12)
TOTAL CHLOROPHYLL (µg/l)	22.9	32.7	37.0	20.8	28.4
CONDUCTIVITY (µmhos)	37,400	33,471	33,650	37,800	35,580
TURBIDITY (NTU's)	4.6	5.0	4.3	2.9	4.2
TEMPERATURE (°C)	22.0	29.0	24.7	15.8	22.9
TOTAL NITROGEN (mg/l)	0.78	1.09	1.13	0.92	0.98

STATION #62   LAT. 27°58'16"   LONG. 82°34'22"

PARAMETER	SPRING (3-5)	SUMMER (6-8)	FALL (9-11)	WINTER (12-2)	ANNUAL (1-12)
TOTAL CHLOROPHYLL (µg/l)	26.0	34.7	38.5	23.4	30.6
CONDUCTIVITY (µmhos)	34,300	30,325	30,517	35,167	32,577
TURBIDITY (NTU's)	6.3	7.1	4.5	4.5	5.6
TEMPERATURE (°C)	22.0	28.6	24.4	15.1	22.5
TOTAL NITROGEN (mg/l)	0.83	1.09	1.13	0.81	0.96

STATION #63   LAT. 27°58'08"   LONG. 82°34'40"

PARAMETER	SPRING (3-5)	SUMMER (6-8)	FALL (9-11)	WINTER (12-2)	ANNUAL (1-12)
TOTAL CHLOROPHYLL (µg/l)	22.3	25.8	30.4	17.5	24.0
CONDUCTIVITY (µmhos)	38,267	36,749	35,383	40,800	37,800
TURBIDITY (NTU's)	4.7	4.9	3.2	2.3	3.8
TEMPERATURE (°C)	22.4	30.1	25.2	16.0	23.4
TOTAL NITROGEN (mg/l)	0.59	0.94	1.04	0.60	0.79

STATION #64   LAT. 27°58'27"   LONG. 82°40'42"

PARAMETER	SPRING (3-5)	SUMMER (6-8)	FALL (9-11)	WINTER (12-2)	ANNUAL (1-12)
TOTAL CHLOROPHYLL (µg/l)	20.7	29.5	31.1	19.9	25.3
CONDUCTIVITY (µmhos)	36,217	33,185	32,350	38,167	34,980
TURBIDITY (NTU's)	5.7	6.0	5.7	3.2	5.2
TEMPERATURE (°C)	21.7	29.8	24.3	14.6	22.6
TOTAL NITROGEN (mg/l)	0.60	0.96	1.15	0.67	0.84

STATION #65   LAT. 27°56'35"   LONG. 82°41'38"

PARAMETER	SPRING (3-5)	SUMMER (6-8)	FALL (9-11)	WINTER (12-2)	ANNUAL (1-12)
TOTAL CHLOROPHYLL (µg/l)	32.4	33.7	37.3	27.5	32.7
CONDUCTIVITY (µmhos)	37,050	34,704	33,150	37,533	35,609
TURBIDITY (NTU's)	7.1	6.6	6.3	5.1	6.3
TEMPERATURE (°C)	21.7	28.7	24.3	15.4	22.5
TOTAL NITROGEN (mg/l)	0.76	1.15	1.23	0.87	1.00

STATION #66   LAT. 27°55'37"   LONG. 82°38'14"

PARAMETER	SPRING (3-5)	SUMMER (6-8)	FALL (9-11)	WINTER (12-2)	ANNUAL (1-12)
TOTAL CHLOROPHYLL (µg/l)	23.5	31.7	34.1	20.3	27.4
CONDUCTIVITY (µmhos)	37,767	35,815	33,883	38,567	36,508
TURBIDITY (NTU's)	5.6	7.2	4.5	3.3	5.2
TEMPERATURE (°C)	21.6	29.0	24.4	15.1	22.5
TOTAL NITROGEN (mg/l)	0.67	0.99	0.94	0.69	0.82

STATION #67   LAT. 27°54'02"   LONG. 82°35'53"

PARAMETER	SPRING (3-5)	SUMMER (6-8)	FALL (9-11)	WINTER (12-2)	ANNUAL (1-12)
TOTAL CHLOROPHYLL (µg/l)	26.4	35.6	31.8	19.0	28.2
CONDUCTIVITY (µmhos)	38,950	37,081	35,433	39,300	37,691
TURBIDITY (NTU's)	4.6	6.6	4.4	3.0	4.6
TEMPERATURE (°C)	21.7	29.1	24.6	15.1	22.6
TOTAL NITROGEN (mg/l)	0.69	0.87	1.01	0.75	0.83

STATION #68   LAT. 27°51'32"   LONG. 82°35'05"

PARAMETER	SPRING (3-5)	SUMMER (6-8)	FALL (9-11)	WINTER (12-2)	ANNUAL (1-12)
TOTAL CHLOROPHYLL (µg/l)	26.1	36.8	34.0	19.7	29.2
CONDUCTIVITY (µmhos)	40,533	39,813	36,833	41,267	39,612
TURBIDITY (NTU's)	4.2	4.7	4.0	2.5	3.8
TEMPERATURE (°C)	21.9	29.3	24.9	15.0	22.8
TOTAL NITROGEN (mg/l)	0.71	0.71	0.95	0.67	0.76

STATION #70   LAT. 27°54'26"   LONG. 82°27'46"

PARAMETER	SPRING (3-5)	SUMMER (6-8)	FALL (9-11)	WINTER (12-2)	ANNUAL (1-12)
TOTAL CHLOROPHYLL (µg/l)	47.5	83.2	53.2	36.4	55.1
CONDUCTIVITY (µmhos)	35,900	32,950	33,100	39,633	35,396
TURBIDITY (NTU's)	5.9	5.4	4.4	5.3	5.2
TEMPERATURE (°C)	22.2	28.9	25.9	17.3	23.6
TOTAL NITROGEN (mg/l)	1.32	1.33	1.52	0.88	1.26

STATION #71   LAT. 27°52'47"   LONG. 82°25'00"

PARAMETER	SPRING (3-5)	SUMMER (6-8)	FALL (9-11)	WINTER (12-2)	ANNUAL (1-12)
TOTAL CHLOROPHYLL (μg/l)	37.4	70.9	36.7	32.4	44.4
CONDUCTIVITY (μmhos)	36,733	36,017	35,500	40,833	37,271
TURBIDITY (NTU's)	14.1	7.7	7.0	9.2	9.5
TEMPERATURE (°C)	22.6	29.8	25.9	17.1	23.9
TOTAL NITROGEN (mg/l)	1.15	1.24	1.29	0.81	1.12

STATION #73   LAT. 27°49'32"   LONG. 82°24'46"

PARAMETER	SPRING (3-5)	SUMMER (6-8)	FALL (9-11)	WINTER (12-2)	ANNUAL (1-12)
TOTAL CHLOROPHYLL (μg/l)	36.7	64.2	35.0	27.4	40.8
CONDUCTIVITY (μmhos)	39,100	39,400	36,333	41,267	39,025
TURBIDITY (NTU's)	7.4	6.8	4.9	4.5	5.9
TEMPERATURE (°C)	22.2	29.7	25.5	17.0	23.6
TOTAL NITROGEN (mg/l)	1.00	1.54	1.40	0.62	1.14

STATION #74   LAT. 27°51'31"   LONG. 82°23'04"

PARAMETER	SPRING (3-5)	SUMMER (6-8)	FALL (9-11)	WINTER (12-2)	ANNUAL (1-12)
TOTAL CHLOROPHYLL (μg/l)	45.4	37.9	38.5	32.2	38.5
CONDUCTIVITY (μmhos)	34,670	37,650	30,967	30,694	33,495
TURBIDITY (NTU's)	6.8	5.4	8.4	5.3	6.5
TEMPERATURE (°C)	23.7	29.5	25.6	16.4	23.8
TOTAL NITROGEN (mg/l)	1.50	1.38	1.43	1.72	1.51

STATION #80   LAT. 27°48'38"   LONG. 82°26'57"

PARAMETER	SPRING (3-5)	SUMMER (6-8)	FALL (9-11)	WINTER (12-2)	ANNUAL (1-12)
TOTAL CHLOROPHYLL (μg/l)	37.0	44.4	32.4	29.4	35.8
CONDUCTIVITY (μmhos)	39,966	40,533	38,000	43,083	40,396
TURBIDITY (NTU's)	6.1	5.6	3.4	4.0	4.8
TEMPERATURE (°C)	22.2	29.6	25.7	17.0	23.6
TOTAL NITROGEN (mg/l)	1.04	0.88	1.16	0.61	0.92

STATION #81   LAT. 27°46'15"   LONG. 82°27'21"

PARAMETER	SPRING (3-5)	SUMMER (6-8)	FALL (9-11)	WINTER (12-2)	ANNUAL (1-12)
TOTAL CHLOROPHYLL (μg/l)	35.3	32.2	27.6	24.8	30.0
CONDUCTIVITY (μmhos)	41,067	41,183	39,133	44,050	41,358
TURBIDITY (NTU's)	6.7	4.7	3.6	3.3	4.6
TEMPERATURE (°C)	21.8	29.4	25.7	16.8	23.4
TOTAL NITROGEN (mg/l)	0.96	0.74	0.93	0.56	0.80

STATION #82   LAT. 27°45'03"   LONG. 82°34'20"

PARAMETER	SPRING (3-5)	SUMMER (6-8)	FALL (9-11)	WINTER (12-2)	ANNUAL (1-12)
TOTAL CHLOROPHYLL (μg/l)	30.8	33.2	26.8	14.9	26.4
CONDUCTIVITY (μmhos)	43,300	41,736	39,567	45,197	42,450
TURBIDITY (NTU's)	4.5	5.6	4.0	3.7	4.4
TEMPERATURE (°C)	22.8	29.7	25.3	16.5	23.6
TOTAL NITROGEN (mg/l)	0.55	0.70	0.84	0.48	0.64

STATION #84   LAT. 27°44'30"   LONG. 82°30'12"

PARAMETER	SPRING (3-5)	SUMMER (6-8)	FALL (9-11)	WINTER (12-2)	ANNUAL (1-12)
TOTAL CHLOROPHYLL (μg/l)	31.5	41.6	30.4	19.6	30.8
CONDUCTIVITY (μmhos)	40,966	41,011	38,767	41,972	40,679
TURBIDITY (NTU's)	6.6	8.5	4.3	4.5	6.0
TEMPERATURE (°C)	22.4	29.1	24.5	16.1	23.0
TOTAL NITROGEN (mg/l)	0.76	0.95	1.45	0.57	0.93

STATION #90   LAT. 27°37'24"   LONG. 82°35'42"

PARAMETER	SPRING (3-5)	SUMMER (6-8)	FALL (9-11)	WINTER (12-2)	ANNUAL (1-12)
TOTAL CHLOROPHYLL (µg/l)	17.2	17.2	20.6	12.4	16.8
CONDUCTIVITY (µmhos)	43,833	48,330	47,433	49,628	48,556
TURBIDITY (NTU's)	3.9	5.2	4.7	3.5	4.3
TEMPERATURE (°C)	22.4	29.5	25.2	16.3	23.4
TOTAL NITROGEN (mg/l)	0.46	0.59	0.58	0.39	0.51

STATION #91   LAT. 27°37'30"   LONG. 82°38'24"

PARAMETER	SPRING (3-5)	SUMMER (6-8)	FALL (9-11)	WINTER (12-2)	ANNUAL (1-12)
TOTAL CHLOROPHYLL (µg/l)	17.7	15.5	20.2	12.5	16.5
CONDUCTIVITY (µmhos)	51,416	49,766	48,967	52,622	50,693
TURBIDITY (NTU's)	4.4	2.1	5.2	4.4	4.0
TEMPERATURE (°C)	22.2	29.7	25.4	16.3	23.4
TOTAL NITROGEN (mg/l)	0.42	0.51	0.61	0.51	0.51

STATION #92   LAT. 27°33'00"   LONG. 82°41'12"

PARAMETER	SPRING (3-5)	SUMMER (6-8)	FALL (9-11)	WINTER (12-2)	ANNUAL (1-12)
TOTAL CHLOROPHYLL (µg/l)	12.3	15.1	18.3	11.0	14.2
CONDUCTIVITY (µmhos)	52,500	52,149	49,833	52,400	51,720
TURBIDITY (NTU's)	4.0	3.2	5.2	3.2	3.9
TEMPERATURE (°C)	22.4	29.6	25.3	16.4	23.4
TOTAL NITROGEN (mg/l)	0.30	0.54	0.58	0.37	0.45

STATION #93   LAT. 27°34'48"   LONG. 82°44'42"

PARAMETER	SPRING (3-5)	SUMMER (6-8)	FALL (9-11)	WINTER (12-2)	ANNUAL (1-12)
TOTAL CHLOROPHYLL (µg/l)	14.9	15.1	18.1	11.4	14.9
CONDUCTIVITY (µmhos)	53,833	52,778	51,967	53,620	53,050
TURBIDITY (NTU's)	4.4	2.3	3.8	4.4	3.7
TEMPERATURE (°C)	22.3	29.5	25.2	16.2	23.3
TOTAL NITROGEN (mg/l)	0.38	0.51	0.66	0.39	0.48

STATION #94   LAT. 27°36'36"   LONG. 82°46'58"

PARAMETER	SPRING (3-5)	SUMMER (6-8)	FALL (9-11)	WINTER (12-2)	ANNUAL (1-12)
TOTAL CHLOROPHYLL (µg/l)	15.2	13.7	17.5	11.6	14.5
CONDUCTIVITY (µmhos)	53,733	52,944	52,800	54,713	53,548
TURBIDITY (NTU's)	6.7	2.4	4.1	5.4	4.6
TEMPERATURE (°C)	21.0	29.4	25.4	16.6	23.1
TOTAL NITROGEN (mg/l)	0.33	0.52	0.41	0.43	0.42

STATION #95   LAT. 27°36'30"   LONG. 82°41'42"

PARAMETER	SPRING (3-5)	SUMMER (6-8)	FALL (9-11)	WINTER (12-2)	ANNUAL (1-12)
TOTAL CHLOROPHYLL (µg/l)	16.9	14.3	18.5	12.7	15.6
CONDUCTIVITY (µmhos)	53,333	51,465	50,633	53,527	52,240
TURBIDITY (NTU's)	5.1	2.1	4.7	5.4	4.3
TEMPERATURE (°C)	22.1	29.6	25.2	16.3	23.3
TOTAL NITROGEN (mg/l)	0.38	0.57	0.48	0.41	0.46

STATION #96   LAT. 27°38'18"   LONG. 82°41'18"

PARAMETER	SPRING (3-5)	SUMMER (6-8)	FALL (9-11)	WINTER (12-2)	ANNUAL (1-12)
TOTAL CHLOROPHYLL (µg/l)	17.6	19.7	22.2	14.4	18.5
CONDUCTIVITY (µmhos)	51,167	49,944	39,807	52,270	48,297
TURBIDITY (NTU's)	5.6	3.6	7.1	4.6	5.2
TEMPERATURE (°C)	22.9	30.1	25.2	16.4	23.6
TOTAL NITROGEN (mg/l)	0.45	0.65	0.85	0.51	0.62

STATION #101   LAT. 28°01'32"   LONG. 82°37'56"

PARAMETER	SPRING (3-5)	SUMMER (6-8)	FALL (9-11)	WINTER (12-2)	ANNUAL (1-12)
TOTAL CHLOROPHYLL (µg/l)	14.7	16.3	23.1	10.7	16.2
CONDUCTIVITY (µmhos)	16,770	16,227	14,872	15,994	15,966
TURBIDITY (NTU's)	7.5	8.7	5.1	4.3	6.4
TEMPERATURE (°C)	22.8	28.3	24.5	15.6	22.8
TOTAL NITROGEN (mg/l)	1.16	1.32	1.22	1.06	1.19

STATION #102   LAT. 28°00'32"   LONG. 82°36'29"

PARAMETER	SPRING (3-5)	SUMMER (6-8)	FALL (9-11)	WINTER (12-2)	ANNUAL (1-12)
TOTAL CHLOROPHYLL (µg/l)	28.2	55.0	47.2	32.9	40.8
CONDUCTIVITY (µmhos)	30,696	25,514	23,737	28,959	27,227
TURBIDITY (NTU's)	6.6	6.1	5.8	5.3	6.0
TEMPERATURE (°C)	23.5	29.4	24.9	15.9	23.4
TOTAL NITROGEN (mg/l)	1.05	0.85	1.27	0.81	0.99

STATION #103   LAT. 27°59'47"   LONG. 82°35'12"

PARAMETER	SPRING (3-5)	SUMMER (6-8)	FALL (9-11)	WINTER (12-2)	ANNUAL (1-12)
TOTAL CHLOROPHYLL (µg/l)	32.3	28.2	21.3	21.8	25.9
CONDUCTIVITY (µmhos)	11,828	10,047	7,242	12,156	10,318
TURBIDITY (NTU's)	6.8	4.9	6.1	6.2	6.0
TEMPERATURE (°C)	23.3	28.2	24.6	16.5	23.2
TOTAL NITROGEN (mg/l)	1.40	1.59	1.37	1.62	1.49

STATION #104   LAT. 27°58'06"   LONG. 82°33'17"

PARAMETER	SPRING (3-5)	SUMMER (6-8)	FALL (9-11)	WINTER (12-2)	ANNUAL (1-12)
TOTAL CHLOROPHYLL (µg/l)	39.0	34.9	30.1	22.8	31.7
CONDUCTIVITY (µmhos)	15,777	8,727	11,289	18,946	13,685
TURBIDITY (NTU's)	8.5	8.3	6.7	6.6	7.5
TEMPERATURE (°C)	22.9	28.1	24.3	16.0	22.8
TOTAL NITROGEN (mg/l)	1.34	1.40	1.26	1.14	1.29

STATION #109   LAT. 27°56'59"   LONG. 82°24'06"

PARAMETER	SPRING (3-5)	SUMMER (6-8)	FALL (9-11)	WINTER (12-2)	ANNUAL (1-12)
TOTAL CHLOROPHYLL (µg/l)	45.7	44.1	32.6	42.9	41.3
CONDUCTIVITY (µmhos)	21,886	23,743	18,973	28,995	23,399
TURBIDITY (NTU's)	3.4	3.9	3.3	3.8	3.6
TEMPERATURE (°C)	23.2	28.8	24.5	15.9	23.1
TOTAL NITROGEN (mg/l)	1.30	1.36	1.49	1.14	1.32

STATION #110   LAT. 27°57'08"   LONG. 82°18'19"

PARAMETER	SPRING (3-5)	SUMMER (6-8)	FALL (9-11)	WINTER (12-2)	ANNUAL (1-12)
TOTAL CHLOROPHYLL (µg/l)	57.6	65.3	36.5	30.2	47.4
CONDUCTIVITY (µmhos)	22,508	26,545	21,328	29,995	25,094
TURBIDITY (NTU's)	5.2	6.7	7.2	3.5	5.6
TEMPERATURE (°C)	24.9	31.0	26.7	18.4	25.2
TOTAL NITROGEN (mg/l)	1.71	1.28	1.39	0.86	1.31

STATION #112   LAT. 27°42'15"   LONG. 82°26'50"

PARAMETER	SPRING (3-5)	SUMMER (6-8)	FALL (9-11)	WINTER (12-2)	ANNUAL (1-12)
TOTAL CHLOROPHYLL (µg/l)	No Data	No Data	No Data	17.1	----
CONDUCTIVITY (µmhos)	20,643	22,927	13,120	17,761	18,613
TURBIDITY (NTU's)	3.8	4.1	3.8	2.9	3.6
TEMPERATURE (°C)	23.8	29.3	25.3	14.7	23.3
TOTAL NITROGEN (mg/l)	1.02	1.16	1.02	0.95	1.04

STATION #114   LAT. 27°51'27"   LONG. 82°16'11"

PARAMETER	SPRING (3-5)	SUMMER (6-8)	FALL (9-11)	WINTER (12-2)	ANNUAL (1-12)
TOTAL CHLOROPHYLL (µg/l)	No Data	No Data	No Data	6.8	----
CONDUCTIVITY (µmhos)	523	463	973	551	628
TURBIDITY (NTU's)	3.0	5.8	3.9	2.9	3.9
TEMPERATURE (°C)	22.3	26.5	23.6	15.8	22.1
TOTAL NITROGEN (mg/l)	2.61	1.91	2.62	2.29	2.36

STATION #132   LAT. 27°50'24"   LONG. 82°20'50"

PARAMETER	SPRING (3-5)	SUMMER (6-8)	FALL (9-11)	WINTER (12-2)	ANNUAL (1-12)
TOTAL CHLOROPHYLL (µg/l)	13.7	11.2	14.9	13.5	13.3
CONDUCTIVITY (µmhos)	391	246	437	522	399
TURBIDITY (NTU's)	4.0	13.2	5.1	5.3	6.9
TEMPERATURE (°C)	20.6	25.4	22.9	14.0	20.7
TOTAL NITROGEN (mg/l)	1.14	1.41	1.24	1.37	1.29

STATION #133   LAT. 27°54'54"   LONG. 82°24'08"

PARAMETER	SPRING (3-5)	SUMMER (6-8)	FALL (9-11)	WINTER (12-2)	ANNUAL (1-12)
TOTAL CHLOROPHYLL (µg/l)	46.9	37.0	32.0	16.8	33.2
CONDUCTIVITY (µmhos)	5,971	6,851	4,421	4,407	5,412
TURBIDITY (NTU's)	8.9	8.0	6.7	4.8	7.1
TEMPERATURE (°C)	21.9	26.8	23.6	14.7	21.8
TOTAL NITROGEN (mg/l)	----	----	----	----	----

STATION #136   LAT. 27°40'30"   LONG. 82°30'15"

PARAMETER	SPRING (3-5)	SUMMER (6-8)	FALL (9-11)	WINTER (12-2)	ANNUAL (1-12)
TOTAL CHLOROPHYLL (µg/l)	28.1	41.5	43.7	42.6	39.0
CONDUCTIVITY (µmhos)	30,377	35,005	24,004	29,446	29,708
TURBIDITY (NTU's)	5.2	6.6	5.6	4.5	5.5
TEMPERATURE (°C)	25.2	30.0	26.1	17.7	24.8
TOTAL NITROGEN (mg/l)	1.26	1.35	1.37	1.29	1.32

MEAN FOR ALL STATIONS:

PARAMETER	SPRING (3-5)	SUMMER (6-8)	FALL (9-11)	WINTER (12-2)	ANNUAL (1-12)
TOTAL CHLOROPHYLL (µg/l)	29.4	36.0	30.8	21.9	29.6
CONDUCTIVITY (µmhos)	36,861	36,102	34,091	38,629	36,420
TURBIDITY (NTU's)	5.7	5.2	4.6	4.0	4.9
TEMPERATURE (°C)	22.4	29.2	25.0	16.2	23.2
TOTAL NITROGEN (mg/l)	0.88	0.98	1.06	0.74	0.92

4.2 APPENDIX B - 1982 COMMERCIAL LANDINGS (POUNDS) AND EXVESSEL VALUES (DOLLARS) FOR SELECTED FINFISH SPECIES FOR PINELLAS, HILLSBOROUGH, AND MANATEE COUNTIES.

The following matrix was compiled from data supplied by Mr. Ernie Snell of National Marine Fisheries Service Office, Miami, Florida, 1984.

Species	Landings (lb)	Study area rank	Exvessel value ($)	Study area rank	Mean Price per pound
Red drum	166,789	5	93,744	6	$0.56
Spotted seatrout	145,925	6	118,943	5	$0.82
Atlantic croaker	12	14	2	14	$0.17
Flounder	18,238	10	11,507	10	$0.63
Pompano	18,920	9	47,363	8	$2.50
Striped mullet	7,184,919	1	1,602,174	2	$0.22
Menhaden	362	13	18	13	$0.05
Sardines	2,283,376	3	189,211	4	$0.08
Grouper & scamp	5,280,830	2	6,441,860	1	$1.22
Jewfish	9,238	12	4,214	12	$0.46
Red snapper	350,135	4	760,175	3	$2.17
Mangrove snapper	72,044	7	92,687	7	$1.29
King mackerel	14,222	11	9,653	11	$0.68
Spanish mackerel	89,206	8	27,911	9	$0.31
Totals	15,634,216		9,399,462		
Average Mean					$0.80

4.3 APPENDIX C - 1982 COMMERCIAL LANDING (POUNDS) AND EXVESSEL VALUES (DOLLARS) FOR SELECTED SHELLFISH SPECIES FOR PINELLAS, HILLSBOROUGH, AND MANATEE COUNTIES.

The following matrix was compiled from data supplied by Mr. Ernie Snell of the National Marine Fisheries Service Office, Miami, Florida, 1984.

Species	Landings (lb)	Study area rank	Exvessel value ($)	Study area rank	Mean price per pound
Clams	70	6	158	6	$2.26
Scallops	1,376	4	3,088	4	$3.24
Shrimp	3,988,435	1	7,975,324	1	$2.00
Blue crab	278,326	2	88,954	3	$1.38
Stone crab	67,368	3	92,663	2	$1.38
Oysters	132	5	167	5	$1.27

4.4 APPENDIX D - COLONIAL BIRD NESTING SITE MATRIX.

Key to Appendix D, Colonial Bird Nesting Site Matrix.

Colony Number - This is the colony number which appears next to the symbol in the atlas.

Colony Type - The colonies in the atlas are type-classed:

        SB = Shorebird
        WB =Wading Bird
        BP =Brown Pelican

FWS Number - The corresponding colony numbers used by the United States Fish and Wildlife Service and the National Audubon Society for larger or less ephemeral colonies are shown in this column. Information concerning colonies without a corresponding FWS number was gathered largely through personal communication with the National Audubon Society and Florida Audubon Society members as well as other published data.

Species Composition:

SB = Shorebirds

AO - American Oystercatcher
BS - Black Skimmer
CT - Caspian Tern
GBT - Gull-Billed Tern
LG - Laughing Gull
LT - Least Tern
NOT - Noddy Tern
RST - Roseate Tern
ROT - Royal Tern
ST - Sandwich Tern
SP - Snowy Plover
SOT - Sooty Tern
W - Willet
WP - Wilson's Plover

WB = Wading Birds

A - Anhinga
BCNH - Black-Crowned Night Heron
CE - Cattle Egret
DCC - Double-Crested Cormorant
GI - Glossy Ibis
GBH - Great Blue Heron
GE - Great Egret
LB - Least Bittern
LBH - Little Blue Heron
TCH - Tricolored Heron
RE - Reddish Egret
RS - Roseate Spoonbill
SE - Snowy Egret
YCNH - Yellow-Crowned Night Heron
WI - White Ibis
WS - Wood Stork

BP = Brown Pelican

Note:
Anhinga and Double-Crested cormorant are not really wading birds but are included because they sometimes nest with wading birds.

(continued)

61

Colony Species	Colony type	Species composition	FWS no.
1	WB, BP	BP, CE, WI, GE, GBH, LBH, RE, SE RCH, BCNH, GE, RS	615007
2	WB	YCNH	615010
3	WB	CE	615011
4	SB	LT	615009
5	WB, BP	BP, CE, GBH, GE, SE	615030
6	WB	GE, GBH, SE	615029
7	WB, BP	BP, GE, GBH, YCNH, WI	615031
8	WB, BP	BP, CE, WI, GBH, GE, SE, LH	615027
9	WB	GBH	615028
10	SB	BS, AO	
11	SB	LT, AO	
12	SB	LT, AO	
13	SB	LG, AO, W	
14	SB, WB	AO, W, GE	
15	SB	W	
16	WB, SB	WI, DCC, YCNH, BCNH, JLH, SE, GE, LBH, GBH, CE, GI, RS, LG, CT, ST	
17	SB	W	
18	WB	CE, SE, WI, GE	
19	SB	WP	
20	SB	LG, BS	
21	SB	LT	

(continued)

Appendix D (concluded)

Colony number	Colony type	Species composition	FWS no.
23	SB	LT, BS, LG, GBT	
24	SB	SO	
25	SB	LT, BS	
26	SB	BS	
27	SB	BS, LG, ROT, ST, LT, AO	
28	SB	LT	
29	SB	LT	
30	SB	LT, BS	
31	SB	AO	
32	WB	LBH, GE, LB, SE	
33	SB	LT, AO	

5. NARRATIVE REFERENCES

Bailey, R.G. 1978. Descriptions of the ecoregions of the United States. U.S. Dep. Agric. For. Serv. Misc. Publ. No. 1391. Washington, D.C.

Causseaux, K.W., and J.D. Fretwell. 1982. Position of the freshwater-saltwater interface in the upper part of the Floridan aquifer, southwest Florida, 1979. U.S. Geol. Surv. Water-Resour. Invest. Open-File Rep. 82-90. Tallahassee.

Florida Department of Environmental Regulation. 1983a. Computer printout of industrial point source discharges in west central Florida. Tallahassee.

Florida Department of Environmental Regulation. 1983b. Computer printout of municipal point source discharges in west central Florida. Tallahassee.

Florida Department of Natural Resources. 1981. Florida recreational guide. Tallahassee.

Florida Department of Natural Resources. 1984. Shellfish harvest area maps (various scales). Tallahassee.

Florida Marine Patrol. 1980. Boater's guide to manatees, the gentle giants. Tallahassee.

Godcharles, M.G., and W.C. Jaap. 1973. Fauna and flora in hydraulic clam dredge collections from Florida west and southeast coasts. Florida Department of Natural Resources, Marine Research Laboratory, St. Petersburg.

Goodell, H.G., and D.S. Gorsline. 1961. A sedimentologic study of Tampa Bay, Florida. International Association of Sedimentology, Copenhagen, Denmark.

Goodwin, C. 1984. Changes in tidal flow, circulation, and flushing caused by dredge and fill in Tampa Bay, Florida. U.S. Geol. Surv. Open-File Rep. 84-447. Tampa.

Hicks, S.D., H.A. Debaugh, and L.E. Hickman. 1983. Sea level variations for the United States: 1855-1980. National Oceanic and Atmospheric Administration. Rockville, Md.

Humm, H.J. 1973. The biological environment. A summary of the eastern Gulf of Mexico, 1973. State University System of Florida, Institute of Oceanography, Tallahassee.

Lewis, R.R., III. 1980. Tampa Bay cooperative seagrass project. Tampa.

Lewis, R.R., III, and R.L. Whitman, Jr. 1984. A new geographic description of the boundaries and subdivisions of Tampa Bay. Mangrove Systems, Inc., Tampa.

Lewis, R.R., III. R.G. Gilmore, Jr., D.W. Crewz, and W.E. Odum. 1982. The fishery resources of mangrove forestry in Florida. American Fisheries Society, Bethesda, Md.

Lewis, R.R., III, M.D. Moffler, and R.C. Phillips. 1984. Seagrass meadows of Tampa Bay-review (draft). Tampa.

McNulty, J.K., W.M. Lindall, and J.E. Sykes. 1972. Cooperative Gulf of Mexico estuarine inventory and study, Florida: phase I, area description. National Oceanic and Atmospheric Administration, National Marine Fisheries Service. Tech. Rep. NMFS Circ. 368. Seattle, Wash.

Moe, M.A. 1963. A survey of offshore fishing in Florida. Great Outdoors Publishing Company. Prof. Pap. Ser. 4. St. Petersburg.

Mook, D. 1971. External morphology and osteological development of the larval and juvenile sheepshead, Archosargus probatocepahlus with notes on its ecology and feeding. M.S. Thesis. University of South Florida, Tampa. 82 pp.

National Ocean Service. 1976. Bathymetric map of St. Petersburg 1:250,000 scale quadrangle. Rockville, Md.

National Ocean Service. 1983. Index of tide stations for the state of Florida. Rockville, Md.

Palik, T.F., and R.R. Lewis. 1984. Southwestern Florida ecological characterization: an ecological atlas. Map narratives. U.S. Fish Wildl. Serv. FWS/OBS-82/47.

Phillips, R.C. 1960. Observations on the ecology and distribution of the Florida seagrasses. Fla. Board Conserv. Prof. Pap. Ser. (2):1-72.

Phillips, R.C. 1978. Seagrasses and the coastal marine environment. Oceanus 21(3):30-40.

Pritchard, P.C.H., ed. 1978-82. Rare and endangered biota of Florida. Vols. 1-6. Florida Committee on Rare and Endangered Plants and Animals. Florida Game and Fresh Water Fish Commission, Tallahassee.

Ross, B.E. 1973. The hydrology and flushing of the bays, estuaries, and nearshore areas of the eastern Gulf of Mexico. Summary of the eastern Gulf of Mexico, 1973. State University System of Florida, Institute of Oceanography, Tallahassee.

Seaman, W., Jr. 1982. Enhancement of Florida marine fisheries using artificial reefs: a review (draft). University of Florida, Florida Sea Grant College, Gainesville.

Slack, L.J., and M.I. Kaufman. 1973. Specific conductance of water in Florida streams and canals. Florida Bureau of Geology, Tallahassee.

Snell, E. 1984. Florida landings - 1982. National Marine Fisheries Service, Miami.

Taylor, J.L., and C.M. Saloman. 1969. Some effects of hydraulic dredging and coastal development in Boca Ceiga Bay, Florida. U.S. Fish Wildl. Serv. Bull. 67(2):213-241.

Wilkins, R.B. 1983. Environmental Quality, 1981, Hillsborough County, Florida. Hillsborough County Environmental Protection Commission, Tampa.

Zieman, J.C. 182. The ecology of the seagrass of south Florida: a community profile. U.S. Fish Wildl. Serv. FWS/OBS-82/25.

6. SOURCES OF MAPPED INFORMATION

6.1 BIOLOGICAL RESOURCES

6.1.1 Approved Shellfish Harvest Areas

Florida Department of Natural Resources. 1984. Shellfish harvest area maps (various scales). Tallahassee.

6.1.2 Oyster Beds

McNulty, J.K., W.N. Lindall, and J.E. Sykes. 1972. Cooperative Gulf of Mexico estuarine inventory and study, Florida: phase I, area description, NOAA Tech. Rep., NMFS Circ. 368. Washington, D.C.

6.1.3 Clams

Godcharles, M.F., and W.C. Jaap. 1973. Exploratory clam survey of Florida nearshore and estuarine waters with commercial hydraulic dredging gear. Fla. Dep. Nat. Resour. Mar. Res. Lab. Prof. Pap. Ser. No. 21. St. Petersburg.

Sims, N.W., Jr., and R.J. Stokes. 1967. Survey of the hard shell clam (Mercenaria campechiensis) population in Tampa Bay, Florida. Fla. Dep. Nat. Resour. Mar. Res. Lab. Spec. Sci. Rep. No. 17. St. Petersburg.

Sprague, M. 1984. Personal communication, discussions of distribution of clams in Tampa Bay and adjacent waters. Florida Department of Natural Resources, Punta Gorda.

Tracy, L. 1983. Personal communication, discussions of distribution of clams in Tampa Bay and adjacent waters. Three T's Clam Company, Madeira Beach.

6.1.4 Finfish Data

Moe, M.A., Jr. 1970. Florida's fishing grounds. Great Outdoors Publishing Company. St. Petersburg.

6.1.5 Shore Birds

Kale, H.W., II. 1978. Birds. Vol. 2 in P.C.H. Pritchard, ed. Rare and endangered biota of Florida. University Presses of Florida, Gainesville.

Kale, H.W., II. Unpublished. Data on selected groups of birds on the gulf coast of Florida.

Nesbitt, S.A., J.C. Ogden, H.W. Kale II, B.W. Patty, and L.A. Rowse. 1982.
Florida atlas of breeding sites for herons and their allies: 1976-1978. U.S.
Fish Wildl. Serv. FWS/OBS-81/49.

Paul, R.T. 1984 Personal communication, nesting sites of shore birds and
wading birds in Tampa Bay. National Audubon Society, Tampa.

6.1.6   Wading Birds

Kale, H.W., II. 1978. Birds. Vol. 2 in P.C.H. Pritchard, ed. Rare and endangered biota of Florida. University Presses of Florida, Gainesville.

Kale, H.W., II. Unpublished. Data on selected groups of birds on the gulf
coast of Florida.

Nesbitt, S.A., J.C. Ogden, H.W. Kale II, B.W. Patty, and L.A. Rowse. 1982.
Florida atlas of breeding sites for herons and their allies: 1976-1978. U.S.
Fish Wildl. Serv. FWS/OBS-81/49.

Paul, R.T. 1984. Personal communication, nesting sites of shore birds and
wading birds in Tampa Bay. National Audubon Society, Tampa.

6.1.7   Manatee Habitat

Florida Marine Patrol. 1980. Boater's guide to manatees, the gentle giants.
Department of Natural Resources, Tallahassee.

6.1.8   Seagrass Beds

Mangrove Systems, Inc. 1980. Seagrass maps of Tampa Bay (scales 1:10,000 and
1:24,000). Tampa.

U.S. Fish and Wildlife Service. 1984. 1982 Tampa Bay NWI update (scale
1:24,000). National Wetlands Inventory Office, St. Petersburg.

U.S. Fish and Wildlife Service. 1982. 1:24,000 scale color photography of
Tampa Bay. National Wetlands Inventory Office, St. Petersburg.

6.1.9   Artificial Reefs

Bureau of Land Management, New Orleans Outer Continental Shelf Office. 1981.
Gulf of Mexico permitted artificial fishing reefs (tracts 67 & 69). New
Orleans, La.

Bureau of Land Management, New Orleans Outer Continental Shelf Office. 1981.
Eastern Gulf of Mexico coastal zone offshore fisheries. New Orleans, La.

Florida Department of Environmental Regulation, Permit Division. 1977. Florida artificial reefs permit notebook. Tallahassee.

Florida Sea Grant College, Marine Advisory Program. 1979. Recreational use reefs in Florida, artificial and natural. University of Florida, Gainesville.

Minerals Management Service, Gulf of Mexico Outer Continental Shelf Regional Office. 1982. Fishery resources - recreation (visual-4, scale 1:1,200,000). New Orleans, La.

U.S. Army Corps of Engineers. 1981. Computer printout of Florida artificial reefs. Jacksonville.

6.2 WATER RESOURCES

6.2.1. Salinity

Hillsborough County Environmental Protection Commission. 1983. Conductivity data for Tampa Bay water quality sampling stations: September 1978 - August 1983. Tampa.

6.2.2 Point Source Discharges

Florida Department of Environmental Regulation. 1983a. Computer printout of industrial point source discharges in west central Florida. Tallahassee.

Florida Department of Environmental Regulation. 1983b. Computer printout of municipal point source discharges in west central Florida. Tallahassee.

6.2.3 Dredge Spoil Disposal Areas

Florida Department of Natural Resources, Bureau of State Lands Management. 1983. Dredge and spoil easement location maps for the southwest Florida area. Tallahassee.

National Oceanic and Atmospheric Administration, National Ocean Service. 1983. Nautical charts: 11410, 11413, 11414, and 11425 (various scales). Rockville, Md.

6.2.4 Tide Stations

National Ocean Service. 1981. Index of tide stations for the State of Florida. Rockville, Md.

National Ocean Service. 1984. Tidal datums for St. Petersburg tide station #8726520 and Clearwater tide station #87267261. Rockville, Md.

6.2.5 Water Quality

Hillsborough County Environmental Protection Commission. 1983. Total chlorophyll, conductivity, turbidity, water temperature, and total nitrogen water quality data for Tampa Bay water quality sampling stations: September 1978 - August 1983. Tampa.

6.2.6. Bathymetry

National Oceanic and Atmospheric Administration, National Ocean Service. 1976. Bathymetric map of St. Petersburg. 1:250,000 scale quadrangle. Rockville, Md.

National Oceanic and Atmospheric Administration, National Ocean Service. 1983. Nautical charts: 11410, 11413, 11414, and 11425 (various scales). Rockville, Md.

6.2.7 Intertidal Zone

National Oceanic and Atmospheric Administration, National Ocean Service. 1983. Nautical charts: 11410, 11413, 11414, and 11425 (various scales). Rockville, Md.

6.2.8 Sediments

Goodell, H.G., and D.S. Gorsline. 1961. A sedimentologic study of Tampa Bay, Florida. International Association of Sedimentology. Copenhagen, Denmark.

Taylor, J.L., and C.H. Saloman. 1969. Some effects of hydraulic dredging and coastal development in Boca Ciega Bay, Florida. U.S. Fish Wildl. Serv. Bull. 67(2):213-241.

6.2.9 Tidal Currents

Goodwin, C. 1984. Changes in tidal flow, circulation, and flushing caused by dredge and fill in Tampa Bay, Florida. U.S. Geol. Surv. Open-File Rep. 84-447. Tampa, Fla.

6.2.10 Freshwater-Saltwater Interface

Causseaux, K.W., and J.D. Fretwell. 1982. Position of the freshwater-saltwater interface in the upper part of the Floridan aquifer, southwest Florida, 1979. U.S. Geol. Surv. Water-Resour. Invest. Open-File Rep. 82-90. Tallahassee.

7. GLOSSARY

alimentary tract - A tubular passage functioning in digestion and absorption of food.

brackish - Pertaining to a body of water whose salinity is between 0.5 and 30 ppt.

carnivore - A meat-eating organism.

crustacean - An aquatic arthropod of the class Crustacea characteristically having a segmented body, a chitinous exoskeleton, and paired, jointed limbs. Examples include lobsters, crabs, shrimp, and barnacles.

detritus - Any particulate organic material derived from the process of decomposition.

dinoflagellate - Minute, chiefly marine unicellular algae of the order Dinoflagellata, characteristically have two flagella and a cellulose outer envelope.

diurnal - Lasting for one day.

forage - To search for food.

gyre - A circular or spiral system of movement, characteristic of oceanic currents.

ichthyofauna - Fish.

isopleth - Contour line connecting points of equal value of a given factor.

invertebrate - An animal species having no backbone or spinal column.

metamorphosis - Marked change in the structure of an animal during normal development, usually in the larval to adult stages. Examples include caterpillars changing into butterflies and tadpoles into frogs.

morphological - The structural makeup of organisms.

omnivorous - Pertaining to an organism which eats both plants and animals.

pathogen - Any agent that causes disease. Examples include viruses, bacteria, and fungi.

pelagic - Pertaining to organisms living in the open water.

phytoplankton - Minute, floating aquatic plants.

piscivorous - Pertaining to organisms that feed on fish.

planktivorous - Organisms feeding on plankton.

planktonic - Pertaining to free-floating microscopic organisms.

spawning - The process of releasing eggs or masses of eggs into the water.

spit - A narrow point of land extending into a body of water.

toxin - A poisonous substance, usually having a protein structure, secreted by certain organisms.

REPORT DOCUMENTATION PAGE	1. REPORT NO. Biological Report 85(15)	2.	3. Recipient's Accession No.
4. Title and Subtitle Tampa Bay Environmental Atlas			5. Report Date December 1984
			6.
7. Author(s) J. Thomas Kunneke and Thomas F. Palik			8. Performing Organization Rept. No.
9. Performing Organization Name and Address Martel Laboratories, Inc. 7100 30th Avenue, North St. Petersburg, FL 33710			10. Project/Task/Work Unit No.
			11. Contract(C) or Grant(G) No. (C) (G)
12. Sponsoring Organization Name and Address National Coastal Ecosystems Team U.S. Fish and Wildlife Service U.S. Department of the Interior Washington, DC 20240			13. Type of Report & Period Covered
			14.

15. Supplementary Notes

16. Abstract (Limit: 200 words)

Biological and water resource data for Tampa Bay were compiled and mapped at a scale of 1:24,000. This atlas consists of (1) composited information overlain on 18 biological and 20 water resource base maps and (2) an accompanying map narrative. Subjects mapped on the water resource maps are contours of the mean middepth specific conductivity which can be converted to salinity; bathymetry, sediments, tidal currents, the freshwater/saltwater interface, dredge spoil disposal sites; locations of industrial and municipal point source discharges, tide stations, and water quality sampling stations. The point source discharge locations show permitted capacity and the water quality sampling stations show 5-year averages for chlorophyll, conductivity, turbidity, temperature, and total nitrogen. The subjects shown on the biological resource maps are clam and oyster beds, shellfish harvest areas, colonial bird nesting sites, manatee habitat, seagrass beds and artificial reefs. Spawning seasons, nursery habitats, and adult habitats are identified for major fish species. The atlas will provide useful information for coastal planning and management in Tampa Bay.

17. Document Analysis a. Descriptors

Atlas, maps, natural resources, conductivity, water quality, habitats

b. Identifiers/Open-Ended Terms

Tampa Bay, point source discharge, shellfish areas, nesting sites

c. COSATI Field/Group

18. Availability Statement Unlimited release	19. Security Class (This Report) Unclassified	21. No. of Pages 74
	20. Security Class (This Page) Unclassified	22. Price

www.ingramcontent.com/pod-product-compliance
Lightning Source LLC
Chambersburg PA
CBHW081230280526
45787CB00006B/2605